WHERE HAVE ALL THE YEARS GONE?

The life, experiences and memories
on both sides of the Atlantic Ocean,
of Silverdale born
Reg. Harvey,
Engineer, Teacher, Entrepreneur.

by

Reg. Harvey

Published by

TCP (Books) Limited

P.O. Box 435 Leek, Staffordshire
England, ST13 5TB
telephone 01538 380910 fax 01538 382204
e-mail: tcpbooksltd@aol.com

ISBN 0 9544080 - 1 - 2

Typeset by Clermont Ferrand Int., Leek, Staffordshire, England
and Printed by J. H. Brookes Ltd, Hanley, Stoke-on-Trent, Staffordshire, England

Contents

Church Street, Silverdale, this photograph was taken in the early twenties.

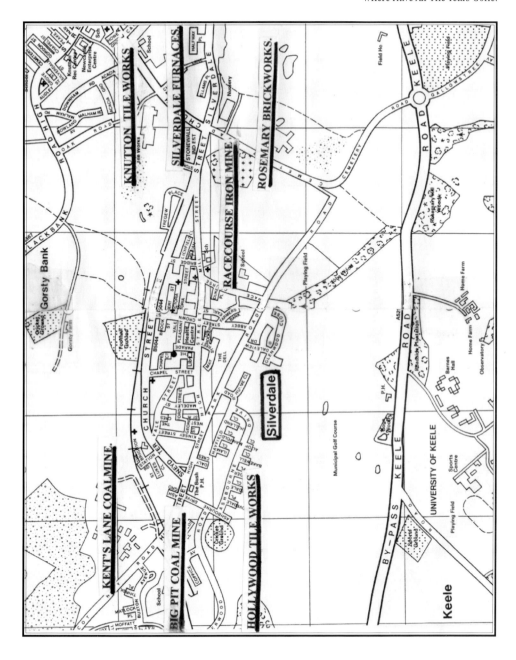

Surrounding the village of Silverdale were numerous brick yards,
iron works and coal mines

Foreword by the Author

As the years unfold, I realise the clock of life keeps ticking. With this realisation I have decided to present my past in order to form a picture of "who I am". From this I intend to reveal the many facets of my character.

When surveying the past, I feel that it is important to go back to birth where it all began. Why we were born or to whom we were born is not a factor when taking our first breath. At this very moment we join the race of time and the formation of 'character' begins.

"Where Have All The Years Gone" is a written testimony (to the best of my knowledge) of the happenings in my life. This is not about my birthplace, the village of Silverdale in Staffordshire England or about the war. It is about the author and all his life experiences.

Dave Adams

St. Luke's Church and village school. The author attended the church and school.
The house in the centre was the headmaster's dwelling.

About the Author

It all started when I was born some twenty minutes after my sister, making me a twin. We were born into a family of four brothers and two sisters. The number of children in our family now totalled eight, and eventually another brother was born. During the time when my mother was giving birth to the twins, her sister died leaving a son, and he also was taken into our family. The family including my parents was now complete, twelve in all.

Our family was poor and the house was small, having two bedrooms in which to house a mixed family of twelve. Father was employed as a low paid labourer at the local mine. Mother's chores, cooking, cleaning, washing and mending clothes were endless with few aids to ease the load. Education for us after the age of fourteen was out of the question. Holding the family together was a priority.

Below
Reg. Harvey
Author, Engineer,
Teacher,
Entrepreneur
Born 1925

Above
Reg. Age 13yrs

Above
Reg. on his
wedding day 1946

Acknowledgements

My sincere thanks go to my patient and loving wife, Barbara, who helped and supported me in writing this book and, as readers of this book will recognize, played an important and active part in my life. My son, Martyn, edited and guided me in the writings. A number of friends read them and encouraged me to keep on writing.

Reg. Harvey, his wife Barbara, son Martyn and grandsons

Courtesy for permission to use photographs and information from their books. Dave Adams; Graham Bebbington; Fred Leigh; Joyce Holliday; Mervin Monk, Computer Graphics, Waterloo University Ontario; Jack Hambling (pit boys waiting for the cage); Thomas Edison Estates, Florida; Gladstone Pottery Museum, Stoke on Trent; Hilary Jackson Lib (general view of Silverdale)

The Gathering Storm

'The Great World War' from 1914-1918 was fought in Europe with Germany against Britain, France, and their allies. The battles were fought in trenches and for the first time tanks and airplanes were used. The long, cold and wet winters took a heavy toll on the soldiers through disease and illness. During the four-year war, millions died and destruction to cities and the surrounding areas was vast.

The following years after the *'war to end all wars'* employment and unrest was prevalent throughout Europe. The world was full of turmoil and ripe for breeding fiends such as Adolf Hitler, Mussolini, Franco and Stalin. Between them starvation, murder and heinous crimes killed over eight million humans.

Britain plans to introduce conscription

"Peace in our time" Britain's Prime Minister Neville Chamberlain returns from a meeting with Adolf Hitler, with a signed document stating that Germany will not occupy any more territories.

Growing Up

Chapter One

Growing Up

Early memories of my oldest sister's wedding are still vividly recalled, being dressed, along with my twin sister, in blue and white velvet suits, at three years old. Family life centred on the church, school, concerts and parties. Growing up included many years being a Cub Scout, Boy Scout and Senior Scout. It also included being a choir member and bell ringer. There was also my first dance and meeting of girlfriends. What happened to all those years? Have they passed by unnoticed? I may not have noticed the years passing, but I have many memories. I recall instances of fighting rival gangs (for no other reason than belonging to the Church of England faith and the rivals were Roman Catholics). Going outside our local area looking for different girls or exploring new scenery was an excursion that could cost us a bloodied nose.

Silverdale, a mining village in the heart of Staffordshire, was recognized as one of the largest villages in England. The population of the village exceeded one thousand, including coal miners from Wales and Yorkshire. People came from all parts of the country seeking employment at the brick or roofing tile works, the coal and iron mines, and the Silverdale furnace.

The Sneyd family of Keele Hall and Heathcote family of Apedale Hall were local industrialists who mined and marketed rich mineral deposits of

View of Silverdale, showing the railway station and Church

Apedale Hall the family home of the Heathcote Family, one of the local industrialist
who mined and marketed mineral deposits from the Silverdale area

the area. Their families prospered from the mining industry and the Sneyds
often entertained world famous people such as members of the Royal family
and Grand Duke Michael of Russia.

Dolly Tub, Mangle and Dolly peg

The small settlement named Silverdale grew rapidly in the early 1900s. Houses had to be built for the incoming workers. These houses were small and built in adjoining rows. They were referred to as 'street houses'. There was no gas, electricity, sewage or running water. 'Out' houses were built away from the main building and were used as 'wash houses' where the family clothes were hand washed. The coal-fired 'boiler' (cast iron pot) heated the water required to bathe or wash clothes. Washing was done by emptying the hot water into a dolly tub where the soiled clothes were placed. The 'dolly peg' (a circular wood disc having five legs attached to a handle) was rotated by hand, one clockwise revolution, then one anti-clockwise revolution repeatedly. This forced the hot soapy water through the clothes. The dolly tub was then placed in position beside the 'mangle' that had two wooden rollers operated by a handle. Wet clothes taken from the dolly tub were passed between the rollers, which then squeezed the water from them.

At the bottom of the garden was the out-house, containing the lavatory that housed the 'ducket'. The ducket was a ceramic-glazed deep basin that collected human waste. Council employees used a special horse-drawn cart to empty the human waste weekly during the night. Communal water taps were later added serving a number of households. Coal gas was used for lighting and heating. Street and roadways began to be paved. This was a vast improvement in the village since the streets had never been paved before. Street gas lamps and sewage drains were installed. In the late 1940s running water, flush toilets and electricity were installed into each household.

In the early 1900s miners rented 'pit houses'. If they lost their jobs for any reason, they had to be out of their home by nine p.m. that day, otherwise, bailiffs immediately removed them and their belongings into the street. In the late 1800s, miners and their families were expected to form a line outside of the church where the men would raise their hats and the ladies would curtsey as the mine owners and their families arrived.

Mining was at the heart of Silverdale's life. The high quality grade coal and deep coal seams made it a profitable venture. It was Kent's Lane Colliery that prospered when other collieries closed down unable to make a profit. My father worked for his entire career as a low paid colliery labourer. He started to work at the age of twelve and retired at the age of sixty-five. He worked a

Kent's Lane Colliery at SIlverdale, a producer of high grade coal.

total of fifty-three years. At the end of his working life there was no pension or golden handshake, only a certificate congratulating him on excellence in good time-keeping and unbroken service to the company. Three of my brothers worked at the coal mine and my three sisters worked in the pottery industry. Shetland ponies, being small in stature and very strong, pulled the coal from the working face to the pit shaft. Once the ponies went down the mine, they never saw daylight again until they were retired after many years of service. The retired ponies were placed in open fields to live out their lives; most were blind because of long periods spent in the darkness of the mine.

Pit Boys waiting their turn to travel down to the coal face in the cage.

As coal was removed from the mine, the ground settled causing the houses above to subside. Many houses in Silverdale and the surrounding area were subjected to subsidence and had to be repaired at the mine owner's cost. At our home in Vale Pleasant, new ceilings and floors had to be replaced. Many buildings had steel cables holding the walls together. Some houses and buildings had to be demolished. Coal was never removed from below St. Luke's Church because it had a tall spire, and doing so would have been dangerous.

Kent's Lane Colliery at Silverdale closed in 1993, due to not making enough profit. It was cheaper to import coal from Australia. Just as hard to believe is that over 30,000 miners lost their lives in the U.K. since records began to be kept in 1850.

Surrounding the village of Silverdale (which was so named because it lies in a valley previously covered with silver birch trees) were numerous brick works, iron works and coal pits. All these industries belched out thick black smoke in competition with the hundreds of 'bottle kiln' (bottle kilns were bottle-shaped ovens where china and earthenware were fired). People employed in the pottery industry are called 'Potters'. Pottery has been produced for over two thousand years. The Roman Empire manufactured clay pottery in many forms, water holding vessels, kitchen utensils, vases and statues. The Potteries is the manufacturing centre in the U.K. Mintons, Wedgwood, Doulton, Aynsley, Coalport, Royal Albert, Johnson Brothers, are just a few of the world famous brands of fine bone china and earthenware produced and sold worldwide.

Staffordshire is rich in mineral deposits, coal, iron and clay. All are

The Bottle Kiln yard at Longton's Gladstone Pottery Museum, now a world famous visitor attraction, during it's working life just another kiln belching out soot-black smoke.

Silverdale Furnaces

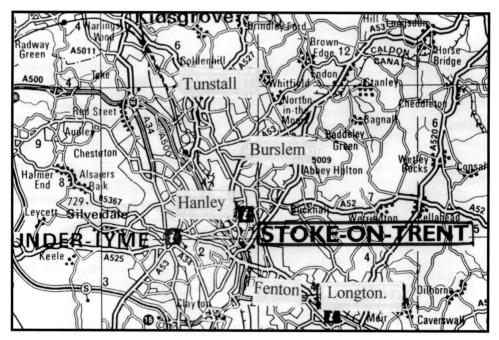

essential ingredients in pottery making. Six towns in the centre of Stafford-shire have become known as the 'Potteries'. They are Tunstall, Burslem, Hanley, Stoke, Fenton and Longton. The well-known local author, Arnold Bennett wrote the novel 'The Five Towns' which is about life in the Potteries. Why he left out Fenton the sixth town is a mystery and gained him much criticism. 'The Card' is the name of a film, which was taken from this novel and featured Alex Guinness. In the Potteries smoke from the bottle kilns blacked out the horizon. The whole area had high mounds of waste known as dirt tips and deep holes called marl holes, which destroyed the beauty of the past landscape. No wonder hundreds of people died of silicosis, a common disease of miners and pottery workers. Tuberculosis, a bacterial disease caused by smog and dust was prevalent. Cigarettes, pipes and cigars filled the air with second hand smoke in pubs and public places. Unknowingly, this helped to spread tobacco-related diseases and shortened people's life span.

The film entitled 'The Proud Valley' featuring Paul Robeson, has scenes taken at Kent's Lane Colliery.

Above: Paul Robeson, star of 'The Proud Valley'

Paul Robeson never came in person to the Colliery. George Bytheway, a Silverdale miner, was a stand-in for him and he was filmed entering the pit cage for descent to the pit. Syd Bebbington, a blacksmith striker at the Colliery and several others were chosen to be film extras. The film depicted the hardships and perils in the lives of miners and their families. Paul Robeson was a world famous black bass singer,

A scene from the film, some of the underground scenes were filmed at Kents Lane Colliery

Syd Bebbington, a blacksmith striker at the Colliery and several others were chosen to be film extras in 'The Proud Valley'.

but, like other black people of the era, had to endure the many injustices of society.

In 1947 after the Second World War, the Labour government passed the 'clean air' bill and coal-fired bottle kiln was replaced with electrically heated kilns. Later coal fires in the homes had to be replaced with smokeless fuel burning fireplaces. (Government grants assisted the cost of this conversion). This changed the Potteries skyline completely and many diseases related to smog and dust disappeared. Many changes took place as people began to recognize that the environment was being destroyed and global warming was occurring. The use of asbestos was banned and lead was no longer added to numerous products such as paint, petrol and ceramic glazes. Having had the knowledge that lead helped to destroy the Roman Empire, why was lead ever allowed to be used?

Silverdale Band c.1900. The Silverdale Prize Band played an important role in the musical life of the village in the early years of this century. They frequently played concerts in the bandstand at Stubbs Walks, Newcastle. Here they are pictured at a seaside location.

Christian faiths organised charities at Eastertime, and church congregations formed processions stopping to sing hymns.

Silverdale was unique in having a church or chapel and pub on every street. These institutions played an important part in village life. Darts and cribbage games were played daily in the pubs. Local bands offered free music lessons from which many became excellent musicians. Christian faiths organized charities at Easter time. Church congregations formed processions, stopping to sing hymns while collections were taken at homes along the way. Children loved to show off their new clothes bought especially for these occasions. Villagers hotly debated which church had the best procession. The 'Annual

Vale Pleasant, looking towards the Co-op on Crown Bank, Joseph Cook was born here in 1860. The author lived at No. 28 by the lamp post on the left.

Carnival' also was an important event for the village and preparations would proceed throughout the year. Competing were 'Morris' dancing groups, Brass bands, Silver bands, and Jazz bands. The instruments played in jazz bands were crude musical instruments made from pipes and funnels. There were decorated floats and individual contestants all competing for top honours. The final event following the awards ceremonies was the crowning of the village queen.

Recalling my past from that era, I think of the hard-working people who made Silverdale village life exciting and who fostered a sense of pride in their community. I remember the Spooner, Wards, and Foster families who organized the carnivals with the help of so many others. Coal-men Jim and Albert

Lee, green grocer Ernie Grafton, and milkman Ernie Hubbard decorated their horses and carts for the occasion. The local Daleians Choir, led by Fred Payne, took top honours wherever they competed. Perhaps the influence of the Welsh miners played a leading part in their success. Spooner's dance hall with its 'sprung' dance floor was recognised as one of the top dance halls in the area. Mr. Fairclough, assisted by Mrs. Lowe, ran a tightly disciplined dance hall. Many American servicemen and young people met their future partners.

Sir Joseph Cook, born in Vale Pleasant in 1860 later to become Prime Minister of Australia. Also pictured left on official duty.

Going to the 'pictures' was a once-a-week treat at the local Roxy (bug hut). Our heroes were Rin Tin Tin, Tom Mix, and the singing cowboy, Roy Rogers. The films broke down several times during each showing because the gas engine would quit. What could you expect for tuppence? Well known figures of our village include Joseph Cook (born in Vale Pleasant, the street where I was born), who became the Prime Minister of Australia, Fanny Deakin, Silverdale's well known local politician, Happy Hampton, local butcher and garage owner, Bonnet's Fish & Chip Shop and bus owner, Podmore's Clothes Shop, and Morrall's newsagent, whose two daughters taught at the local schools. For

Silverdale Scout Headquarters built with the untiring efforts of Reg. Harvey's brother, Cyril.

those who worked at Kent's Lane Colliery, the name Jimmy Beardmore will bring back memories. Visiting the local doctor meant an appointment with either Doctor Daley or Doctor Johnson, who were both village doctors for many years. Elsie Ashley, born in Silverdale and worked in the Newcastle Co-op shoe shop, was in local politics for more years than I can remember, eventually becoming the Mayor of Newcastle under Lyme. My brother, Cyril Harvey, brought Scouting to high recognition in Silverdale and the surrounding district. Building a permanent Scout headquarters was the result of his untiring efforts. Becoming a member of the Scout movement which Lord Baden Powell started in the year 1907, makes one a part of a worldwide family. Silverdale's scout troop collected scrap metal, waste paper, and cardboard during the war years. They also were active in fire-watching duties, Red Cross and St. John's Societies. A

Albert Street. T. W. Carryer and Co. a pawnshop managed by Mr. J. (Jim) Watson was also a general clothing and boot store. It was at this pawn shop that the author, as a boy, took 'dad's' blue serge suit every Monday and received two shillings and three pence then collecting the suit back on Friday for a payment of two shillings and six pence.

number of Scout members lost their lives during active service in the armed forces. Staffordshire achieved international recognition for the Scout movement having visitors from many parts of the world attending the Kibblestone Camp. C. Marshall Amor started the camp in 1927 and later became full time secretary of Stoke-on-Trent Boy Scouts' Association and camp warden.

In my family, work chores were passed down from senior to junior children. As I matured, so did my chores - from washing dishes to turning the clothes mangle handle on washing days. Of course, there were 'lad' jobs, such as carrying coal from the outhouse, and there were 'girl' jobs such as ironing and making beds. One mature job, which I dreaded, was taking Dad's 'best' blue serge suit every Monday morning to the local pawnshop. The suit would have to be collected back from the pawnshop on Friday. The pawning of Dad's suit was kept a secret from him because only the poor resorted to this lifestyle. He was so proud, that starvation would have been more tolerable to him. When I look back at this period of my life, it appears 'unplanned', although the life did make a man or woman of each of us.

Can any school beat Knutton Modern Senior School's total of eight sets of twins? Here they are commencing front row: Joyce and Eric Hill, Patty and Betty Barrow, John and Jyce Latham, Fred and Alan Ford, Molly and Eli Beeston, Ethel and Agnes Webb, Reg and Margery Harvey, and Lily and Arthur Williams.

Our family attended the Church of England. Therefore, we went to St. Luke's Church School, while other denominations attended the Council School. At the age of eleven years, all elementary male students who gained entry to high school education chose Newcastle High School or Wolstanton Grammar School. Female students who gained high school entry attended the Orme Girls' High School. Those who had not gained high school entry went to Knutton Modern School for a period of three years, leaving school at the age of fourteen.

'Pop' Woolley was the head master during the time that my twin sister and I attended the school. Other teachers were Miss Morral, Mr. Burrows ('Killer'), Jimmy Cork, Mr. Speed, Miss Barnish, Mr. Porter and Miss Tittenser. The school was 'mixed' having both boys and girls in the classes. Three hundred and fifty students attended the school. Amazingly, in our class year we had eight sets of twins (four sets of opposite sex twins and four sets of same sex twins). Students were graded into 'A', 'B' and 'C' classes. Punishment (referred to as 'having the stick') was graded in 'one stroke', 'two strokes', 'three strokes', and 'four strokes', depending on the severity of the miss-deed. Being late for school, talking in class, fighting, telling lies, swearing, copying other student's work, and bad writing were reasons for punishment. From the teachers listed above, it is obvious who 'dished' out the best strokes. Female teachers sent students to male teachers for punishment.

Although I did not know it, my character was being formed as an entre-preneur. I cannot recall making the conscious decision to improve my lot in life, but my mother was a great influence on me, urging further education as the recipe for self-improvement. (Martin Luther King, the black leader in America, urged all his brothers and sisters to pull themselves up by their boot straps).

My entrepreneurial skills began early in my life. Gathering leaf mould (rotten leaves for the garden compost) from local woods was hard work but neighbours willingly paid pennies for a sack full. Repairing broken toys, bicy-cles, and many other household items resulted in monetary rewards. A coat of paint worked wonders.

England's King George V and Queen Mary were approaching their 'Silver Jubilee'. The heir to the throne was Edward, the Prince of Wales, who would become King Edward VIII. Edward met and fell in love with a married lady, Mrs. Simpson, who was an American. She later divorced. This created a con-troversial issue. Later, refusing to give up his new found love, he was forced to abdicate in favour of his younger brother who became George VI. The world was in turmoil in the early 1930s. Germany's Adolf Hitler, Italy's Mussolini, and Spain's General Franco were all dictators, who kept themselves in power by eliminating all opposition. The three dictators were preparing to take over adjoining countries by force in order to expand their own empires. 'The gath-ering storm' was building over Europe.

Germany's dictator, Adolf Hitler along with his Henchmen, Goering, Himmler and Goebels planned their future course. Their plan was to create a 'Super Race' consisting of white healthy Germans and those who did not fit the standards would be eliminated. Germany would take over all adjoining countries and eventually world domination. It occupied Austria, then Czecho-slovakia. Britain and France sought assurances that no other countries would be occupied. In August 1939 Britain's Prime Minister Neville Chamberlain returned from a meeting with Adolf Hitler, with a signed document stating that Germany would not occupy any more territories. Chamberlain, upon returning to the U.K., waved the agreement and called out 'we have achieved peace in our time'. A few days later Hitler unleashed his already planned vicious attack on Poland. Sunday, September 3, 1939, Chamberlain sent a message to Germany, stating that if they did not cease the attack on Poland by eleven a.m., Britain would declare war on the Reich. Receiving no reply, Cham-berlain announced over the radio 'Britain was now at war against Germany'. The gathering storm had broken over Europe.

Vickers Spitfire Mk1 goes on show to the press for the first time at Eastleigh Aerodrome in Southampton. The new fighter is fitted with a 12 cylinder liquid-cooled Rolls Royce 'Merlin' engine, the exact horsepower of which cannot be revealed for defence reasons, but there is no doubt that this is the Royal Air Force's most powerful weapon.

Starting to work in the coal mine at the age of fourteen years certainly sped up the growing process. It was immediately apparent to me that working down the coal mine was not for me. Once a week I would not report for work but go the to the local Rolls Royce factory to apply for an apprenticeship in Engineering, which had now become my ambition. Rolls Royce Company personnel assessed that my education standard was too low for an apprenticeship, but each week I would apply hoping that I might get lucky.

After several weeks, I was being reprimanded for my persistence when a gentleman carrying a briefcase inquired about the problem. After being briefed, the gentleman agreed to interview me. He was the tool-room supervisor. When the interview was completed he gave me his decision. I would be given an apprenticeship on condition that I would attend evening school in order to obtain 'O levels' in English, Mathematics, Drafting, and Science. Ordinary level in education was the level reached for those attending high school and this commitment meant three nights a week for three years. I agreed.

Reginald Mitchell C.B.E. The 'Spitfire' plane designer was born in Butt Lane, Stoke-on-Trent.

When I informed the colliery personnel I was leaving their employment, I was told that mining was a wartime priority and I had to stay. A friend worked in the colliery office and between us devised a scheme. I would go to another colliery to seek employment and obtain a note stating that I had been given a position of employment with them. Changing employers within the trade was allowed. Presenting the note at the colliery office, my friend gave me my release papers. Upon arriving at Rolls Royce with my release papers, I began the career that was my ambition. I felt so proud and determined to succeed.

Alas, my problems were not over. Eight weeks after commencing my apprenticeship, I received a government letter asking me why I had not reported to the colliery and asking where I was working. I was ordered to appear before a tribunal. My Rolls Royce supervisor agreed to attend the tribunal with me but could not promise to be successful in convincing them to allow me to stay on at the Rolls Royce Company. Tears rolled down my cheeks when the tribunal announced that I would be allowed to stay. The next two years were

very difficult for me and many 'hard knocks' had to be endured. My English homework was deemed unacceptable because the writing and spelling were poor. The Mathematics homework proved too difficult and I needed a lot of help. Growing up (or maturing to use a more appropriate word) is different for each of us. Life's early experiences, the ones we thought passed unnoticed, mould our character and give us strength to fight the hard knocks of life. Good family life and love are essential ingredients to our future success. Weaknesses and strengths are prevalent within us all. I learned that persistence was my strength and this would help me to achieve my goals.

Chapter Two

Passing Years

Three years passed and my apprenticeship was nearing the halfway point. Seven years was the required time to obtain the status of 'Journey-man'. War was raging and Britain was now alone in the fight against Nazi tyranny. Doom and gloom fell upon us all but from these depths emerged a voice, which eventually led us to victory. The voice was that of Winston Churchill, the wartime leader of Britain.

WInston Churchill. Britain's war time leader and hero.

Winston Churchill took over the leadership of Britain from Neville Chamberlain. Both were members of the Conservative Party, which was in power in 1939. Neville Chamberlain resigned from the leadership of the party for health reasons. Chamberlain was a weak leader and it was obvious that he was not suitable to lead Britain to victory. Churchill on the other hand was recognised as a tough fighter, not only in deeds, but as an outstanding orator. His many famous wartime speeches rallied the British people to arms and determination to go forward to victory. The most famous speech was "We shall fight on the beaches. We shall fight on the landing grounds. We shall fight in the fields and streets and in the hills. We shall never surrender". It was Churchill's tenacity that gave rise to the saying 'British Bulldog'.

People in occupied countries risked imprisonment or death, just for listening to Churchill's broadcasts. The American nation admired Churchill as one of their own (Churchill's mother was an American citizen). American Presi-

Franklin Delano Roosevelt. Thirty-second President of the United States of America

dent Roosevelt, a staunch supporter of freedom, became a close friend of Churchill and the British people. Later, British and Americans fought side by side. Millions of oppressed human beings will be forever indebted to Churchill and Roosevelt.

In the 1920s the British Empire had a strong influence on world policies. The empire, which later became the Commonwealth, included Canada, Australia, India and many smaller countries. The world atlas showed two-fifths coloured red, these areas denoting the British Empire. Hundreds of thousands, both men and women, came to defend Britain in its darkest days from all parts of the Empire. Thousands died or were wounded. Britain is forever indebted to the Empire, for without these brave men and women our freedom would have been lost.

The Rolls Royce Company was given the task of developing a secret weapon under the guidance of Group Captain Whittle. The secret weapon was the 'Jet Engine'. Urgency demanded that the factory be on full continuous production.

The Battle of Britain was being fought in the skies over Britain and many died each day. Britain's most famous fighter plane, the 'Spitfire', maintained Britain's air supremacy. Germany's fighter plane was no match for the Spitfire. Reginald Mitchell, designer of this famous plane, was born in Butt Lane, Stoke on Trent, and a plaque denotes his birthplace. At the start of the Battle of Britain the R.A.F. had only 600 aircraft, mainly Spitfires. Germany had over 3000 combat planes. Britain had developed 'Radar' and much to Germany's surprise the Spitfires were always lying in waiting no matter where they planned their attacks. Radar was unknown to Germany at that time. Even in darkness the German losses out-numbered those of the R.A.F. The word spread that the R.A.F. pilots were eating lots of carrots, which helped them to see in darkness. When the Battle of Britain ended, the Luftwaffe had lost 1,733 planes and many of their finest pilots. R.A.F. losses numbered 915 planes. Most of the pilots parachuted to safety.

This photograph show Newcastle-under-Lyme High Street. 'The Old Town Hall', 'The Stones', the original 'Castle Hotel Building' and lots of 'Shoppers'

In the factories, production committees were formed to find ways to increase production and watch for absenteeism. On what appeared to be a normal workday, we received a message from the shop steward to stop production. It was customary for operators of grinding machines to drink a pint of milk each day to prevent damage to the lungs caused by dust. Milk was in short supply, so the canteen personnel mixed water with the milk to make 'Hot Chocolate'. This had been done without the Union's permission. Several of the toolroom staff, including myself, refused to strike and a week later we were summoned to a union tribunal and sentenced to 'Coventry' for three months for disobeying the union strike call. Being sent to 'Coventry' meant that our fellow workers were not allowed to speak to us and of course many unpleasant instances occurred.

Working hours at the factory were long, seven a.m. to seven p.m. every day for one month, changing to seven p.m. to seven a.m. alternatively. The night shift was useful as my older brother had a taxi business, and due to the war-time restrictions, he had to work at the colliery. During the night-shift periods I was available to assist in keeping the business going.

The Japanese bombed Pearl Harbour on the 7th of December 1941. This ended the isolationist forces in America in wanting to stay out of the war. Tokyo announced that Japan was now at war against the U.S.A. and Britain. Britain was no longer alone in the fight for freedom. The build-up of American forces began taking place throughout Britain. The tremendous task of bringing 750,000 American troops into Britain meant building large numbers of troop-carrying ships and naval craft to defend them against 'U' boats. The battle of the Atlantic was very costly to the allies both in ships and human lives. The Queen Mary was fitted out to carry 5,000 troops, from the U.S.A. to Britain. Amazingly, she suffered no losses or damage. With her speed she could outrun the U-boats.

Many thousands of American service personnel were camped in Staffordshire and two local estates, Nelson Hall and Drake Hall, became base for them. These two estates were twelve miles from the nearest town and local taxi services were called upon to transport the American service personnel each day from the bases to town. I arrived at Drake Hall base to pick up soldiers and drive them to town and to my amazement all the soldiers were black. I had never seen a real live black person before. A list of local 'Pubs' was given to the taxi drivers, which later became known as the 'Black Pubs'. No white Americans were allowed to go to them.

Nelson Hall was the base for white American soldiers and they had to be taken to the better class 'White Pubs'. The racial situation was bewildering to the local people who queried "Are they not all human beings fighting for freedom"? It was sometime later that I learned about the racial situation that existed in America in the 1940s. Black people had to ride in the back of public vehicles and they were not allowed to stay in better class hotels, or attend white schools, colleges and universities. They were second class citizens. Many of these injustices have been corrected. Dr. Martin Luther King was a black leader who led the fight against these injustices. He was against all forms of violence and his protests were in the form of non-violent marches. He was assassinated April 4, 1968 at one of these protest meetings.

One day upon arriving at one of the bases, all taxi drivers were called to a meeting. The purpose of the meeting was to discuss cab fares. The American soldiers thought that the seven shillings and sixpence fare was for each person and not the full car fare. In future we were to charge that fare for each soldier. It would benefit us to fill the car to capacity. Having eight or more people in a five-seating cab made driving hazardous. One such hazardous trip comes to mind. I had eleven soldiers in a seven-seating cab speeding down a steep incline, which had a sharp right-hand turn. I was negotiating the bend too fast and mounted a grass slope. The car was now speeding and inclined at forty-five degrees. Woeful cries echoed within the disarranged car interior, but luckily I was able to right the car and come to a halt. Two soldiers, pale and shaking, asked "How far is it to town"? I told them about two miles. Paying the full fare, they decided to walk the rest of the journey. One of the soldiers (who had leaned his head into the open car window) commented "I was over Berlin last night and it wasn't this ***!!! rough".

Continuing my apprenticeship as a tool and die maker taught me many facets of engineering, lathe work, milling-machine work, fitting, and precision grinding. Attending evening school year after year increased my self-esteem and confidence. I now had my eyes set on higher goals. Pleasures in life evolved around Scouting. Many of the young people who would have been present in peace times were in the Armed Forces. I was asked to become a scoutmaster of a nearby scout troop. It was at one of those weekly meetings that I met a young lady, who later became my wife. At one of the weekly meetings a young Canadian soldier visited us. He was with the Canadian Forces based close by. His name was Alan Pearce from Ontario, Canada and he was active in the Scout movement. Alan attended our weekly meetings and assisted in the training of our youth. He became a close family friend and at my mother's invitation spent weekends and leaves at our home. During one of the meetings Alan told us all Canadian Forces were going to be confined to camp. We learned later of the Dieppe raid in which so many brave Canadians died. The raid was deemed a disaster. Alan died in that raid. Our family and the Scout troop lost a true friend, and we never said our good-byes. Perhaps the Dieppe raid on August 19, 1942 was the forerunner of the allied landing which followed later, the raid in which British, and Free French troops assisted the main Canadian force who carried out the assault. Casualties sustained by allied forces were heavy. However, the raid did bring to light many lessons that had to be learned for the future invasion of Europe.

Working long hours at the factory gave us little time for other activities, although I enjoyed 'Roller Skating' at the rink in Hanley and recall joining in the 'whip', which to beginners was a hair-raising experience. The 'whip' was a long line of skaters who 'snaked' around the ring at very fast speeds. All skaters were expected to join in, otherwise one was looked upon as being a 'chicken'. Travelling had to be by bus, as car owners were not allowed any petrol.

Rationing was introduced in December 1940. Butter (four ounces) and bacon (four ounces) were the first followed later by sugar (12 ounces), meat, chocolate, tobacco, cigarettes and clothes. Queuing (lining up) for food rations became a common scene in this period (food rationing ended in 1945). If it became known that a shop had extra food available, there would be a race to join in the line-up. I recall the occasion when it became known that a contraband shipment (contraband refers to a captured enemy ship's cargo being distributed to the public free of charge) of bananas were located at Betley railway sidings. Several brothers and myself cycled to Betley and collected several stalks of bananas. Our family lived on bananas for the next few weeks. People cycled from miles around in all directions, but of course the return journey meant walking. The stalks, which would be up to six feet long and covered completely with dozens of bananas, were very heavy and had to be supported on the cycle's handlebars and seat.

The Government encouraged people to grow their own food and allotments were made available at low cost. Other schemes devised were to rear chickens for food and to produce eggs. If one chose to rear chickens, the egg ration was forfeited but you kept the eggs that were produced. Rearing two pigs was allowed; when the pigs reached ten score in weight the local butcher would slaughter them and buy one and a half pigs from the family, while the remaining half pig was kept for family consumption. Again one forfeited one's meat allowance. Whether this encouraged a 'black market' was debatable. 'Black Market' was obtaining extra rations above the allowed rations. If one could not eat all the pork on hand, why not exchange the pork to the coalman for some extra coal? Our family kept chickens and two pigs. To enable one to collect 'pig swill' (stale bread, potato peelings, etc.) from the neighbourhood, two gallons of petrol per month was allocated. A 1938 Morris 8 h.p. car was used to collect the swill. The rear seat was removed and a new galvanized dustbin placed in the back. I learned to drive the car, enabling me to collect the swill. Driving tests had not been introduced at that time. After the war, if one had driven for several years without any accidents a driver's license was issued to you.

At the height of the air attacks, large cities in the south of England evacuated young children to smaller towns in the north of England. Silverdale was the home for many evacuees. One and a half million children were evacuated. The day the children were evacuated they went to school with a change of clothing, toothbrush, comb, gas mask, and a bag of food for the day. Fleets of buses took them to main line railway stations. Trains travelled north to different cities. Parents waited several days to hear about their children's location.

The German Luftwaffe bombed British cities, airfields, factories, and railway stations. I recall seeing distant lights and flashes in the night sky. It was Coventry being razed, including the Cathedral. Over one thousand civilians died in the one night raid. Several days later I drove some neighbours to Coventry and took part in a funeral for their relations. I learned later that Churchill had been warned that Coventry was Germany's next target. He had to keep the secret because if it had become known that the raid was expected, the source from where it came would be revealed and that source could not be lost. The Potteries had few air raids and these often were by lone plane attacks. Crewe Railway Station and the Rolls Royce factory were regular targets, but suffered little damage. The defences for Crewe were 'barrage balloons, search lights and naval guns'. The naval guns when fired rattled windows in Silverdale, which was twelve miles away. The searchlights gave spectacular night shows. Barrage balloons were balloons in the shape of Zeppelin airships. These were attached to long steel cables and surrounded the area that was to be protected. Their purpose was to stop low-level air attacks on the target.

Britain became a large fortress with thousands of men and women including soldiers, airmen, and naval personnel from the Commonwealth, Free French, Dutch, Polish and Americans, all waiting for the invasion of Europe, but air superiority had to be won if victory was to be accomplished. When air superiority was accomplished then the task of destroying Germany's war machine was carried out. Nightly one thousand bomber raids began systematically destroying German cities. When the 'softening up' process was completed (softening up refers to rendering the enemy to a position where they are unable to defend themselves), the invasion of Europe was launched June 6, 1944.

The allied landings took place on June 6, 1944. This was called 'D-Day'. An armada of landing craft, mine sweepers, and war ships went into action. Thousands of human beings from both the allied and axis forces died. The allies at this time had air superiority. This helped to make the landing in Europe successful. The race to destroy the V2 rocket-launching sites was top priority. The Nazi forces under pressure on both the Soviet and allied fronts began to crumble. Only then did the horrors of the Nazi death camps come to light. The horrors were beyond comprehension. How any human beings could take part in such hideous degradation is unbelievable. Adolf Hitler and his fellow fiends were in the process of eliminating all Jews, Gypsies, and Polish Nationals. Tears still roll down my cheeks when I recall the Ann Frank story. How many similar stories could be told? Amazingly, many of the butchers escaped justice and lived out their lives unpunished.

Germany was finally defeated on the 7th of May, 1945. Most of its cities reduced to rubble and millions of human beings killed or maimed. Europe was free for the first time since 1939. War in Asia was in progress with fighting taking place in many different areas. Malaya, Burma, and Singapore had to be won back. The Japanese war came to an abrupt end when the Allies dropped the world's first Atom Bombs on the 6th of August 1945 on Hiroshima, followed on the 9th of August 1945, on Nagasaki. Emperor Hirohito of Japan surrendered unconditionally. The price of victory for the allies was 55 million dead.

With the end of the German war, the emergency wartime rules were relaxed. At Rolls Royce all military-aged personnel were instructed by the government to report for National Service Duty. National Service Duty was for a period of eighteen months. This would enable wartime personnel to be demobbed. I was told to report to R.A.F. Padgate, Warrington, Lancashire.

Chapter Three

Living Years

My National Service was short term compared with those called up at the outbreak of the war. Many served six or more years, whereas my service was for eighteen months. National service consisted of basic and trade training. Basic training taught discipline, marching, and the use of firearms. My trade training was engine maintenance. R.A.F. Cosford near Wolverhampton was the engine training school. It was only thirty-five miles from my hometown. On 'off-duty' weekends I would 'hitch-hike' home. Wearing a uniform made hitchhiking easy since truck drivers and motorists were eager to give Service Personnel rides.

Arriving back at the camp one Sunday evening after spending a weekend at home without permission, my companion and I made our way around the perimeter fence in darkness, where we recognized the unofficial camp entrance and proceeded to crawl through the bushes and under the fence. Dusting off our uniforms, we were confronted by lights, excited police dogs, and military police. We were taken to the official camp entrance where we found ourselves standing to attention outside the guardhouse in quick time. Standing to attention for long periods of time is very exhausting with the corporal yelling down our ears and demanding our response loud and clear "I am an idiot' or "I am not a human being', which had us trembling in our boots. It was a relief to be marched into the commander's office to be sentenced and reprimanded. We were sentenced to one hundred and sixty-eight hours without pay in the Camp Detention Centre.

While serving time there, every step taken is at the double. The day starts with a cold shower at 5:00 o'clock a.m., followed by inspection and thirty minutes of double marching, finally followed by breakfast. I recall my first working day (8:00 a.m. to 6:00 p.m.) moving a high mound of coal from one end of the storage yard to the other end, by wheel barrow, at the double, then scrubbing the concrete floor where the coal had previously stood. After lunch the coal had to be moved back to its original place and the concrete floor swept and scrubbed clean. One hundred and sixty-eight hours was a long time.

After my trade training I was sent to an airfield in Norfolk where I worked on 'mothballing' Mosquito aircraft. Mothballing aircraft consists of removing ignition parts, spark plugs, etc. and greasing moving parts. Many of these

B.S.A. Rolls Royce, Rists. Second World War technology led to the setting up of mechanised production lines, which were devoted to the mass manufacture of one or two components only. Numerous production lines would feed large scale sub assembly and final assemby plants.

The B.S.A. Gun Company was bombed out of Birmigham in 1940 before their Newcastle factory was ready. An agency factory making parts for aircraft cannons for them had been approved in 1939, but was not brought into operation until April 1941. Rolls Royce, already in the area at Fenton and Stoke, took over the B.S.A. factory in 1944 to increase capacity. When Rolls Royce vacated the plant in February 1946 it was taken over by Rists, who remain there, albeit in a very different guise, until the present day.

planes had been involved in famous dog fights and secret reconnaissance missions. During my R.A.F. Service I married Barbara. Shortly afterwards, my National Service ended and I was 'de-mobbed' and returned to civilian life.

Previous employers had to re-employ de-mobbed service personnel and I returned to Rolls Royce. Many changes took place. Rolls Royce closed down their local factory. Rists Wire and Cables acquired the factory and most of the former employees remained employed. Since Tool and Die Makers manufacture jigs, fixtures and dies for all trades, my skills did not have to change. My previous toolroom foreman Maurice Abberley had left the employment of Rolls Royce and started a company designing automated pottery machinery. Later his company Malkin Engineering Co., located in Chadwick Street, Longton approached me with a job offer. My new work would be working with a team designing a new cup-turning machine and other products. Studying new methods of production for the pottery industry was essential to meet the new era in which global competition would have to be met to survive.

Accepting the job offer, I joined the engineering team and worked on the automated cupturning machine. Many problems had to be overcome. The first machine was to be installed at the famous Minton Pottery Company. On arrival we were confronted with a stone-throwing angry crowd. The trade union said that automated machines were a threat to their membership livelihood. The new cup-turning machine would do the work of four tradesmen and produce cups near to perfection using unskilled labour. The team along with the cup-turning marvel retreated back to its place of birth. Eventually an agreement was reached with the unions. Only cup-turning trades-people would operate the machines. The machine was installed with resounding success, resulting in many orders for the cup-turning marvel.

Later I was sent to service a cup-turning machine and much to my surprise, some ladies in the clay department used language that sent my neck hairs bristling. But more was to come. While I was working on the machine, I was suddenly pulled to the ground, my pants removed by several ladies and wet clay rubbed on what previously had been my 'private parts'. I was assured that I was now initiated and accepted into the fold. On the ladder of hierarchy, the clay department was not on the top rung and 'hazing' (being initiated) was common practice.

At this time Barbara and I were living with my parents, who were alone now that my twin sister was forced to leave home. It had become known that she was pregnant. On learning this fact, my father refused my sister entry to our home again. She had nowhere to go, but the disgrace she brought upon the family earned her no sympathy. Ironically, years later after my mother passed away, my father became critically ill with cancer and required full-time care over many months, and it was my twin sister who cared for him. Later in life I regretted the fact that I did not stand by my sister, insisting that if she goes, then so do I.

Taxi driving was still a part of my life and the money would help to build up a deposit for a home. The taxi was old and spare parts difficult to obtain. Breakdowns were a common occurrence. I recall an incident when a neighbour was extremely distraught because his daughter was pregnant and was to be married at the local church. He booked our taxi for the occasion. I arrived at the home and switched off the engine, which was a mistake. The bride and her father proudly got into the car and I proceeded to start the engine. The starter whirled and whirled but the engine refused to start. The bride's father was upset at this embarrassment, especially as the crowd of well wishers grew in numbers. I tried to calm him down and assured him that a push start would do the job. The crowd of well wishers was eager to oblige. My instructions to the pushers were to "get a good run, then I will put the car in second gear and release the clutch'. Off we went and soon the pushers were yelling "now, now!' I engaged the clutch; the whole car jumped and shook the bride and the unborn baby violently. I realized that I had not turned on the ignition key, but kept this to myself. I assured the brides father that two push starts were quite common and away we went, ignoring the "now, now ' calls in order to get a good speed before releasing the clutch. When the speed was right, I turned on the ignition. The passengers were warned of the upcoming event, then in went the clutch. There was a loud explosion that the whole village heard. The tyres squealed, black smoke billowed at the rear and the well wishers scattered. The car shook at every firing of one or maybe two cylinders. I was relieved when the engine gave up because the back-firing and shaking was not how the wedding car should arrive at the church, which was now in sight. The well wishers again determined to see the job through, got the car rolling again and the journey was over. It was quite obvious to me that I was in the father's 'bad books'. He ordered me (not requested) to see that another taxi would be waiting to return them home after the wedding and to not expect to get paid. 'The baby girl was born prematurely but in excellent health'.

Barbara and I worked hard to earn extra cash. Driving the taxi enabled us to look for a house to purchase. A small house located outside the village became available. It had two bedrooms and was very small with an outside wash house and toilet. There was no electricity or gas and the toilet had to be emptied, but the house was our castle.

The first morning I was roused from my sleep with "This is the B.B.C. 6:00 o'clock news'. Upon investigation, I found that my next door neighbour had the windows wide open and the radio at full volume. I assumed this was an isolated event but each morning I would be awakened to hear the news one hour earlier than I desired. I approached my neighbours very cautiously, not wishing to upset them. I requested that they turn down the volume on their radio, only to learn the scorn of a lady's tongue. Talking to other neighbours about this, I was told that the radio affair had gone on for years and watch out for the wife, who was vicious. I made one more attempt to right the matter and of course the viciousness worsened. I was now determined to accept the challenge. I had observed that 9:00 o'clock p.m. was their 'bedtime', and I devised a plan to place my motorcycle in a corner against the wall under their bedroom window and run the engine at full volume. This would awaken the dead. Allowing twenty minutes for my neighbours to sink into deep slumber, the plan went into operation and it was a resounding success. Looking up at the open bedroom window, I could see but not hear the neighbour's wife commanding me to turn off the *** ! ! ! engine. After what appeared to be a lifetime and knowing that both of my neighbours were fully awake, I retired to wait the next move.

After waking up to the alarm clock, it was some time before I realized the normality of the situation but as I wheeled my motorcycle to the front of the house, the normality ended abruptly. A screaming, ranting form appeared. I was jumping and ducking to avoid vicious broom blows. These blows stirred my adrenaline, locking both of us in a fight for the broom. Winning the broom battle, I proceeded to break it into many parts and hurled them across the highway into the field opposite. I was warned that her huge husband would settle the score that evening.

Later that morning I related to my work-mates the disastrous events that had taken place. The overwhelming opinion was that I should be made ready for the upcoming onslaught.

At lunch hour, boxing gloves were chosen for me but after several boxing bouts, it became obvious that I was not the favourite to win this big fight. To stand a chance of surviving this contest, biting, scratching, screaming or going for private parts was my only hope. An hour after arriving home, I decided to show myself in the garden. The suspense had become unbearable. After a few moments (my heart pounding within my chest) I heard my neighbour's door open and a roaring voice called out "hey bastard, I want a word with you'. In a flash I leaped on the wall screaming "nobody calls me a bastard'. I was dumbfounded to witness my neighbour turn and run into the house, closing the door behind him. Why I did not accept his humiliation, I will never know. I chased him to the closed door, fists clenched, beckoning him to come out and fight. Luckily for me, he declined, ignoring his wife's remarks of cowardice and demands to get out there and "kill him'. It was over (for me at least). I had survived quite well and I never heard the 6:00 o'clock news again.

Viewing Silverdale from 'Stone Wall'. The road on the right, Newcastle Street, leading to Church Street. Kent's Lane Colliery Tip is in the background. The houses on the right were built on Silverdale's White Star Football Field. The road to the left is Mill Street, leading to High Street. The first house on the right of Mill Street is the 'Swan Hotel'

Above and Left

2nd November 1949.
Princess Elizabeth visits
Enderly Mills which produced
uniform clothing for the armed
forces, police and firemen
during the war.

Britain was now in a recovery period and industry was booming. The desire to improve my financial position was strong. I decided to take a chance and become self-employed, leasing a small workshop and machinery, with money borrowed from my father. A promissory note to repay the loan by monthly instalments was signed and I left the employment of the Automated Ceramic Machinery Company.

The next few months were tough; no salary, no orders, and I had difficulties repaying the loans. Barbara was now the sole salary-earner, but we were both determined to make the venture work. Later I met a new friend named 'Vin' who required help in designing and manufacturing new equipment for the flat roofing trade. Unfortunately he too had no funds available and depended upon his wife's earnings for their livelihood. Our friendship bonded and our businesses grew as a result of this bonding. There were times when I required help, just as there were times when he required help. This two-way support was always there and this friendship has lasted throughout our lives.

In 1950 I decided to take a chance and become self employed, renting a workshop in London Road, Trentvale.

Where did the years go? Unexpectedly, I learned that the lease on the workshop I was using would not be renewed. At this time I had been offered a full-time teaching position in drafting, machine shop and woodworking. My education certificates were high enough to admit me into teaching, but to be granted a full qualification certification, I had to obtain one 'A' level certificate, the subject 'English Literature'. Making my decision, I accepted the teaching position and transferred my Engineering business to my friend's business premises. My entire production at that time was roofing equipment for 'Vin', therefore, I could work during the weekends in the business while my nephew took charge during the week. The new arrangement was very successful and new employees were required to meet production demands.

On the first day of my teaching assignment, I arrived at the school carrying a brand new briefcase. A driver of a bread van stopped me in my path. The driver who I recognised from my school days asked me where I was going. I said that it was my first day as a teacher at the school. He expressed his surprise and pointed out that he was an 'A' level student and I was a 'B' level student. How did I get the job as a teacher? I explained to him, that after leaving school I had attended evening school for further education courses for a period of sixteen years. My first day as a teacher began a career which would span thirty-five years.

Broadmeadow Secondary Modern School, Chesterton 1957 Teaching Staff.
The author is seated front row extreme left.

Back Row left to right: - Roy Brain, Garry Nicholson, Stuart Lee, Dennis Grocott, Keith Jackson, Ken Bateman, Maurice Steele, Arthur Henshall, Geoff Heath.
Front row left to right: - Reg. Harvey, Hartley Bailey, Colin Marks, Bill Philbin, (Assistant Head), Brian Toms (Headmaster), Arthur Lawton, Alan Thomas, Harold Lea, Maurice Wade.
Broadmeadow was a Seconday Modern School for boys, with all male teaching staff. Subjects taught were: English, Mathematics, History, Geography, Science, Physical Education, Woodwork and Metalwork. In 1957 corporal punishment was being phased out. (There was opposition and concern, over the loss of discipline in the classroom and school).

To change from industry to education took time, patience and learning. The fifties in Britain brought about many changes in education including the abolishment of corporal punishment. Teaching of trades became a part of the curriculum. I soon realized that imparting knowledge to others required special skills. Respect had to be earned, caring was a two-way direction and most importantly, a little humour added icing to the cake. A serious gang problem was evolving in some of the youth and became known as 'Teddy' Boy behaviour'. I first encountered such behaviour whilst on yard duty. I noted two students dragging another student towards an outhouse. I hurriedly followed them and witnessed one student holding the victim in an arm lock while the other student spat into the victim's face. A surge of rage befell me and I manhandled the perpetrator between a milling mass of students to my classroom and dealt him two of the best strokes of the cane. I found out that the victim had not paid his weekly protection dues to the 'Teddy' boy gang who were collecting large sums of money from the student body.

Later that day the school principal sent for me and proceeded to show disapproval at my disgusting behaviour. He handed me a note from the boy's father stating that he would be waiting for me at the end of the school day. I asked the principal if he was interested in the details of the happenings but he continued to rant, so I walked out of his office only to have him screaming at me to return. He threatened that I would be 'fired'. I ignored his demands, returned to my classroom and sent a student to bring the perpetrator to me. When he arrived I asked him why he did not bring his father's note to me since it was addressed to me. Giving him another stroke of the cane, I told him to inform his father I would be waiting for him at the end of the school day. I then told him to go to the principal's office and relate to him what had taken place. Much to my surprise the boy's father did not arrive and I did not lose my teaching position. In fact I became a hero for the staff and students.

Observing behaviour I noted that childhood environment teaches and moulds character. The reason human beings have short fuses, violent behaviour and anti-conformity can be traced back to their early life experience. It would be wrong to assume that only negative learning takes place. Love, caring and conformity are positive and lasting lessons. A teacher's behaviour has positive or negative influences on students.

A number of happenings required decisions. Barbara's father passed away. My friend, 'Vin' had located a piece of land that was suitable for the building of two homes. He urged me to join him in purchasing it and build us new houses. As he was in the building trade, we would have many advantages. Barbara and I decided to sell our country home and live temporarily with her mother. We would then purchase the land and build the houses.

The next two years were very busy. No holidays or weekends off and lots

Vin had located a piece of land that was suitable for the building of two homes.

to learn. I became a 'Jack of all trades'; carpenter, bricklayer, electrician, roofer, painter and most importantly, odd job man . Many family members joined my team and we became known as the ' weekenders. What a wonderful feeling and how proud I was of our achievements especially when the house was completed and we moved in. One year later our son was born. Where have all the years gone? We had been married nine years.

No holidays or weekends off and lots to learn

When 'Vin' and I were working on the homes we noted that a large amount of rubbish was being dumped on our property each night. We decided to work late in the evening in order to watch for the culprit. Working quietly, Vin drew my attention to a figure in the darkness dumping a wheelbarrow of rubbish on our property. It was a neighbour who lived opposite and was doing repair work on his home. We were very surprised because he was a general manager of a well-known soccer team. He had an immaculate garden, at least until we quietly returned all of the rubbish to his front lawn. That was the end of the dumping and any chances for free tickets to soccer games.

The following nine years in our new home was wonderful. Setting trees, flowerbeds and garden paths transformed the wastelands into a beautiful garden.

The following nine years in our new home were wonderful. Walking to school, planning the garden with a fishpond and watching our son grow up in a safe environment. This period was marred when one of the most revered people in my life died. This person was my mother. The sorrow that befell family and friends left deep scars upon all our hearts. Among her many triumphs were the following: raising nine children, rearing her younger sister when her own mother died and also raising another sister's orphaned son. My father should also be credited because he agreed willingly to all the arrangements relating to the family matters. On no occasion did my mother lose her temper or complain. She never had a holiday apart from visiting her younger sister whom she had raised, and who lived in Preston, Lancashire. Her aim in life was to encourage all her children to educate themselves. Not all heeded but were no less loved. Traditional Christmas days brought all the family together for a party, attended by as many as thirty adults and children. Several sittings were necessary while the mounds of food were devoured. A life long regret for Barbara and myself is that we never 'got on our feet' in time to give our parents the many things they did not have. (Getting on our feet is a term given to the time in our life when we become financially secure.)

Our friends, Vin and Betty had two boys and a girl. Living next door to each other, our family bonds grew tighter. I recall a water-meter inspector coming to check for a watermain burst, and noticing the fishpond, he became interested in the source of water used to fill it. I proceeded to show him the wonderful idea Vin and I had, stating that all the rainwater coming from the roof was directed to the pool; hence we did not have to pay for the water. Some time later I received a bill for the pool water, which had to be paid annually. I destroyed the bill but some time later a demand for immediate payment arrived. Again I destroyed it thinking that someone had made a mistake. Later I received a notice to appear in court for non-payment of the water. I went to my lawyer to explain the mix up and he produced an old law book that stated that Henry VIII deemed all water (including rainwater) in the royal Realm belonged to the crown and had to be paid for. I promptly paid up.

I was kept busy over these nine years, full time teaching and working weekends at the engineering company. There were few holidays and these were often marred by rainy weather. Britain's weather can be wonderful but overcast wet weather is prevalent. How quickly the years pass. I had been teaching five years at my first school when a friend from my apprenticeship days approached me to join him at the local Further Education College and become an assistant lecturer in engineering. I accepted the position and eventually after several promotions became a senior lecturer. This promotion placed me in charge of a school that had thirty lecturers and several hundred students.

Lecturing senior students was very different for me. There were undoubtedly fewer discipline problems but preparation was required. Many of the students at the college were on day release from company apprenticeship schemes. Attending college one day a week was compulsory for advanced practical courses. The London City and Guilds Institution set courses and examinations.

Living in the house for nine years, friends and enemies are made. Surprisingly, some neighbours never get to be known, not even their names. Being a part of a community can become your life. Many people become involved in the church, dancing or crafts. There are many different interests, painting, quilting, woodworking, model making and of course all the sport activities. Barbara's interest was in keep fit activities and we enjoyed dancing and walking, but finding time to do the activities of one's choice demands loyalty and commitments. The reward and friendships are immeasurable.

Making friends or enemies in a community often occurs in a spontaneous way and is not planned. Arriving home from school one day I was met by Barbara, who was very upset because our four year old son had stepped in some dog droppings while playing in the front of our home and had walked on the carpet badly marking it. I was aware of an inconsiderate neighbour who walked his dog each evening allowing it to ' poop' on the pavement[1] in front of our house. The following evening I waited and watched. Sure enough on the identical spot the dog left its droppings. I approached the dog's owner, suggesting that he clean up the mess. He ignored me and walked on. The following evening the performance was repeated. This time I warned the dog's owner that I would take drastic action if the mess were not removed. Again I was ignored. The time had come for 'action' or 'clean-up'. The nightly performance took place. Once again I approached the dog's owner requesting he remove the droppings because I would no longer tolerate having to clean up his dog's mess. Of course he was unaware of my intentions and continued on his way. I brushed up the droppings onto a dustpan, walked up to his house and rang the doorbell. When his wife answered the door, I emptied the contents of the pan into their hallway. The dog's owner did not walk his dog past our home again, nor did he become a friend.

The theme of my life seems to be 'change' or, as my mother-in-law often referred to my character, 'restless'. During the nine years in our new home, a number of changes took place. This period of our lives was a test of endurance. Our son, Martyn attended a nursery school located close to the school where I taught and the hardware shop we had purchased. Barbara and her mother managed the shop and I assisted them after school hours cutting glass, trimming wallpaper and delivering heating oil to customers. The heating oil was stored in a five hundred-gallon tank in the yard. I installed pipes from the tank to the building enabling me to fill a twenty-gallon drum from which the ladies could serve customers. When I came in from school I would refill the drum, which always took a long time taking me away from other important chores. Consequently I would often leave the drum filling while I went away to tend to other things. I recall on one occasion getting involved cutting glass! And then being called to the shop for advice. It was perhaps one hour later that my mother-in-law asked me where the heating oil drum was. The back room where the oil was filling was a step down. The over-spill oil filled the room to the top of the step. I spent the next few hours filling all the hollow vessels I could find.

The district where I lived had; 'poor' 'middle' and 'rich' class areas. Driving through the rich area one day, I noted a piece of land, which appeared to

---

[1] Sidewalk - For the benefit of those living on the other side of the Atlantic

be vacant. I made inquiries and found that the land was situated on a beautiful wooded hillside that had been quarried for stone many years ago. I was assured that the site was unsuitable for the purpose of building a dwelling place. This was the only vacant site in the area. I made many visits to the site and approached the owner about buying the land. He was amazed that anyone would want to buy the land. I eventually purchased it for a third of its value and later built my dream house for a cost of six thousand pounds. Twenty-five years later the house was placed on the market for two hundred and fifty thousand pounds.

More decisions were made. We would sell the hardware business, take a much-earned vacation and visit my brother who had immigrated to Canada a number of years ago. Having sold the hardware business we arranged our vacation to Canada for the month of August 1960, which was the school summer break. Martyn was now five years old and very excited at the prospect of going to North America on H.M.S. Queen Elizabeth. Our passage was booked aboard the Queen Elizabeth for the outward journey and the Queen Mary for the homeward journey. Arriving at Southampton docks, the vastness of the Queen Elizabeth was breathtaking. The last time we had sailed was to the Isle of Man on the 'King Orri', a flat-bottomed boat. I doubted if the King Orri could have supported one of the Queen's funnels. After walking up the gangway, we waited in line to meet the ship's captain. It was tradition for him to greet everyone with a handshake and then have a steward carry the passenger's luggage to his or her cabin. Moving forward in line and presenting our boarding tickets, we were redirected to another officer, who after welcoming us aboard, directed us to a stairway that led to our cabin. We carried our luggage down many flights of stairs and decks where another steward met us. "Do we have a port hole in our cabin?", I asked. "No sir, you are below the waterline". Later I learned that travelling economy class, which cost three hundred and fifty pounds (a fortune to us) made us the poor relations, hence you carried your own luggage and used stairways. After all, first class passengers paid one thousand pounds for their passage.

Leaving Southampton that Tuesday evening with many fanfares, we sailed to Cherbourg, France to pick up more passengers. Our cabin was rather small and cramped. There were bunk beds on which to sleep. The food was excellent, provided you felt like eating, as seasickness was very prevalent. Sight seeing various parts of the ship, spending time on the open deck, swimming, dancing and taking part in organized activities kept us very busy. One night I was awakened by a loud whirring noise which seemed to go into the distance and then return. It continued throughout the night. I was told later by the steward that the ship's stabilisers that come into operation in rough seas caused the noise. Stabilizers are long threaded rods having centrifugal weights that travel up and down them. When the ship lists to one side, the stabilisers open doors to compartments allowing water to fill or empty them, adding or lowering weight to either side of the ship, thus stabilising it. The size of the ship's

The Queen Elizabeth arriving in New York. New York's skyline was breathtaking with all the skyskrapers, Statue of Liberty and many famous ships. Silverdale's Skyline was in a different world.

The Statue of Liberty set on her own Island, in New York Harbour 'The Lady With The Lamp' is the symbol of freedom and a welcome to America. It was erected in 1886. All the great passenger liners, and millions of immigrants pass this huge welcoming statue.

R.M.S. Queen Elizabeth (top photo previous page) 83,673 tons, built in 1940, 1031ft long 118ft wide. Carrying 2283 passengers from Southampton to New York, a distance of 3,000 miles in four and a half days at speeds of 28.25 knots per hour. Eventually she was sold and moored in Hong Kong, where she caught fire and sank.

R.M.S. Queen Mary (above) 81,000 tons, built in 1935, 1018ft long 118ft wide. Carrying 2139 passengers on the Atlantic runs at speeds of 28.5 knots per hour. Converted to a troop carrier during the Second World War, carrying 16,000 GI's each crossing. In 1967 sold to become an hotel in California.

---

funnels, decks, dining rooms, swimming pools and banquet halls was truly amazing. On a calm day the ship's wake could be seen for miles. It is incredible how the propellers can give the ship such tremendous speed of thirty-five knots (forty miles per hour).

Arriving in New York at six a.m. the following Friday morning and passing the Statue of Liberty will always be remembered. (The Statue of Liberty was presented to the American Nation by France and had to be towed across the Atlantic Ocean). My brother, wife and son met us at the New York docks. The drive to Toronto through New York and the Catskill Mountains was beautiful and breathtaking.

During our holiday we visited Niagara Falls with its indescribable view and its unsurpassable beauty. The gardens, parks and buildings are most fitting to the natural surroundings. Over a million visitors from all over the

The first white man to discover Niagara Falls was Father Louis Hennepin, in 1678.
Today 12 million visitors annually, from all parts of the world, come to see nature's
marvel. Niagara Falls is known as 'The honeymoon capital of the world'.
In 1901 Annie Taylor aged 63, was the first woman to go over the falls in a barrel and
survive, a number of males and females have tight rope walked over the falls.

world come to see this wonder. Lovely continuous sunshine and the outdoor
living gave us the holiday of our lives. Toronto and Ottawa, the capital of
Canada, are beautiful cities and noted for their cleanliness. Returning home
on the Queen Mary was just as enjoyable, sailing through the channel into
Southampton makes one realize how much activity takes place around these
small islands. Our friends back home must have become tired of hearing our
never ending stories. Back home after our Canadian vacation, I was set to
build our dream home amongst the local millionaires. Barbara was concerned
how I could find the time to build the house. It took two years to build and
many 'locals' were amazed that ordinary people were able to tackle such a
huge project.

During this time, Barbara's mother suffered health problems and it became clear that she could not live alone. I persuaded her to come and live with us by promising that I would add extra rooms to the building that was in progress. These rooms would give her complete privacy. She agreed and the arrangement turned out well. Materials required to build the house were more available than in the previous decade. Many improvements in designs and building materials were taking place. The war had been over for fifteen years and wartime regulations and shortages were a thing of the past. The house was designed with changes from the 'norm' taking into account the houses I

had seen in Canada. Of course, a 'patio' had to be included. The weekenders commenced by clearing the trees and brush where the house was to be built. Next came the digging of the 'footings', using spades. A footing is the term used for the trench that will house the concrete base on which the house stands. The trench has to be a minimum of three feet deep, reaching solid

On the picture on the right, the small boy on the right is Jonathan Bartholomew

ground. I had to deepen the trench to six feet in some places.

The 'weekenders' were again fully engaged building my dream home. I had to leave home at 7:00 am to collect the weekenders and drive them to the site, aiming for an 8:00 am. start for work. Two pounds cash was paid for eight hours work. Tradesmen contracted for their rates of pay. For instance, the bricklayer charged ten pounds for laying one thousand bricks, which he expected to do in eight

Previous page
and this page:

The
'Weekenders'

hours. He was recognized as the best bricklayer in the village and would only do the expertise part of his trade. Mixing cement and stacking up bricks was not a part of his job, but it had to be approved by him. Stacks of bricks had to be positioned along the trench at precise distances. If the distance deviated, his trowel would be thrown down amid threats of resigning, which often occurred. His usual complaint was that he had to stretch too far for a brick and if that occurred a thousand times, he would be 'buggered up' before the end of the day. The term 'buggered up' means 'too tired to work'. The trowel would go down if the brick 'frogs' were not facing upwards (the term frogs refers to the hollow side of the brick). Chants of ('frogs up') came from the young stackers when placing the stacks. Arguments would break out between the stackers and the bricklayer who was accused of always moaning and having the easiest part of the job. He retorted that they had bricks in their heads instead of brains. The teatime break always bonded them back together with "you're not bad lads" and "sorry about always moaning, I get out of bed the wrong side on Sundays".

The dream house progressed in spite of being 'rained off' many times. Priority was given to getting the building 'roofed in', and then the inside work could proceed during the winter months. Inspection of the building takes place at different stages as the house progresses. On one occasion the drains were being inspected and the inspector found a blockage in one of the drain runs. 'Will I have to dig up the entire drain run to locate the blockage?', I inquired. With a knowing smile the inspector fetched from his car two thin copper plated welding rods, which had two inches bent at an angle of 90 degrees on one end of both wires. Loosely holding the wires between his thumb and forefinger, he pointed the wires away from him and proceeded to walk along the drain run. Suddenly the wires moved together. He indicated that this was the blockage position. Seeing the look on my face, he assured me that he had located the blockage. Digging down, sure enough, there was the broken drainpipe.

One day, as I was driving my car in the pouring rain along the lane leading to the building site, I saw a gentleman walking and I offered him a ride, which he accepted. I asked him where he was going and he answered that he was on his way to a building site to inspect a bungalow roof, which he called a monstrosity. Knowing that my building was the only one in progress, the monstrosity roof was mine. I wondered if I should drop him off and disappear for a while

At last, the Dream Home finally finished 1962

or stay and witness his embarrassment. I stayed and all went well. I recall working late one Sunday evening, with the disgruntled weekenders who complained about the time, stating that it was too late to start laying roof boards and much too dark for the job. Convincing them to stay a little longer, we proceeded to lay the boards. Some time later I tripped and fell through an opening. There was great elation. It was the answer to their prayers, "now we can go home" and when I had recovered, all the weekenders had their coats on. Leaving the roof unfinished, I drove them home despite my wounds. The building progressed, thanks to the weekenders and shortly my dream home was completed. Moving out of our first home brought sadness, leaving a neigh-bourhood and friends. Moving into the country dream home amongst the millionaires provided me with years of landscaping tasks. The property was one acre of wooded hillside and included a large valley of full-grown silver birch trees. The house was situated at the top of the valley and looked directly over the birch trees and across the Cheshire plains. The site was a landscap-er's dream. Eventually I had an outside swimming pool and fishpond with a waterfall cascading down into the valley. The next period of our lives was most enjoyable, living in a beautiful home, watching Martyn and his friends playing in the swimming pool and the surrounding woods. I was working on the landscaping and enjoying every minute of it.

The engineering business now named 'Hotfast Roofing Equipment Com-pany' was growing fast and it became clear that we required a larger building. I approached my bank manager, requesting a loan of thirty- thousand pounds to purchase the land on which to build a new workshop. I informed the bank manager that I would be building the new workshop with the help of my employees, The Weekenders. The bank manager agreed to my request, but required my house deeds as collateral along with monthly payments over a five year period. Work commenced on the new building. My time again was fully occupied with my daytime lecturing position, working Saturdays at Hotfast, and Sundays on the new workshop. Using the 'Weekenders', the building seemed to appear overnight. The new workshop had an office, canteen, wash-

Using the "Weekenders", the building seemed to appear overnight. The new workshop had an office, canteen, washrooms and a small retail shop, a new venture that became very successful.

rooms and a small retail shop, a new venture that became very successful. My nephew managed the business and Barbara managed the office and book-keeping. The business continued to grow and new commodities were added.

Two years later I was summoned by my bank manager, who informed me that the government (which was in serious financial difficulties) had issued instructions on small loans and house mortgages.

The orders mandated that loans up to fifty thousand pounds had to be recalled within six months and new house mortgages must have twenty-five percent deposit. It was clear that I was in grave financial difficulties. I was unable to borrow the money from banks, family members or friends because of the uncertain future. Loan sharks were not considered. Six months quickly passed and again I was summoned to my bank manager's office. He informed me that my dream home would be put up for auction. I pleaded with him for more time without avail and the house was sold with two months vacant pos-session. The money from the house sale cleared the loan and the engineering business was secure. I was left with four thousand pounds. Finding another house without a mortgage for four thousand pounds appeared impossible. Driving through a middle class area one day I came across a gentleman erect-ing a 'For Sale' sign in his front garden. I approached him to ask about the sale. He informed me that unless I had the cash to cover the purchase, he would not talk about the sale. I assured him that I had the money available. He was asking four thousand five hundred pounds for the house. He asked me for my bank's name so that he could confirm my statement. The next day having been told that the money was available, he invited Barbara and I to view the property. Many structural changes were required in order to suit us, but the house was in good condition and in a most desirable area. We agreed to purchase, promising to pay half the purchase price the next evening and full settlement when the lawyer completed the sale.

The next evening an unexpected problem arose. Another person had ear-lier made arrangements to purchase the house, but had not secured a bank loan. Two months had passed without contact, therefore, the house owner decided to advertise the property. The original purchaser was furious and insisted that the house was his, now that he had secured a loan. The vendor and his wife who were in their eighties, were very distraught. I suggested that we let the house owners have time on their own to decide who would be the lucky buyer. I was very happy to receive a telephone call later that evening, informing me that I had been chosen to purchase the house.

Once the house was purchased we had several weeks in which to carry out our structural changes. Again, the weekenders went into action. Five coal-burning fireplaces were removed. The dining room was separated from the sitting room by a dividing wall, and this wall was removed. An inside 'coal house' became a washroom and the removal of another wall made the kitchen larger.

Central heating, double-glazing the windows, new floors or carpets and complete house decoration had to be carried out in quick time. Working long hours on the house every evening and weekends enabled us to be ready for the move and a date was set for a Monday morning. During the final week prior to moving, I developed a toothache. A wisdom tooth was removed on the Friday morning. Time was running out and work con-

The house was in good condition and in a most desirable area, but required many structural changes to suit our requirements

tinued. Lots of work organizing the dream home for the upcoming move and making ready the new home to move in. I was in pain but pain-killing tablets enabled me to carry on. On Sunday Barbara, Martyn and I were kept extremely busy cleaning and packing at two homes ready for the move the next morning. The pain grew much worse and I was unable to open my mouth. I could only use a straw to take liquids. At six pm. I was in extreme pain and had to be taken to the emergency department at the local hospital. A surgeon examined me and informed me that I had 'Tetanus' (lockjaw). I was to be admitted immediately and an operation was scheduled for six am. the next day. I informed the surgeon that I would not be available, explaining to him the situation, but he interrupted abruptly in a loud voice saying, "You will be dead in twenty-four hours, young man. I will reschedule the operation for tomorrow morning at nine am. Be here.'

At 8:30 am the following morning, the moving van drove out of my dream home driveway and off to the new home. Barbara also drove out of the driveway, but her destination was to deliver me to the hospital. After the operation, the surgeon informed me that he had removed all of my top and bottom teeth on the right hand side of my mouth, assuring me of a full recovery. I was released a few days later, minus twelve teeth. Barbara and Martyn had already unpacked our belongings and settled in by the time I finally returned to our new home.

For several years Britain's economic situation slumped, unemployment increased and business at 'Hotfast' slowed down. Martyn's senior school term was coming to an end. Soon a decision would have to be made regarding his future career and which University he would attend. Discontentment, which started when our dream home was sold, had increased, making the Canadian prospects look good, especially knowing a lecturing position was assured. The decision to emigrate to Canada was made and plans to sell our house and 'Hotfast' went ahead. If I had known about the consequences of our decision to emigrate, and the shock waves that would travel through our family, friends and business acquaintances, I am sure any thoughts of emigrating would have been abandoned.

More thoughts and consideration should have been given to the decision to emigrate to Canada at the age of fifty. The old adage "Hindsight is twenty, twenty vision" is very wise. At the age of fifty years there has been a 'lifetime' making friends, business acquaintances and enjoying strong family bonds. Consequences of emigrating are only realized in later years. The bond of family love is tested by the distance of three thousand miles. It is most apparent when a family member passes on leaving those behind to grieve. The distance prevents activities which are often taken for granted, such as dropping in for a cup of tea, or to simply 'pass the time of day'. Indeed the decision to emigrate certainly did have implications and consequences.

Toronto, with a population of 2,000,000 is the 13th largest metropolis in North America. It is recognised for its beauty, cleanliness and as a safe city. Toronto is a modern city with Lake Ontario waterfront, underground transport system, the worlds largest free standing structure, namely the C.N. Tower (Canadian National), zoo and International Airport.

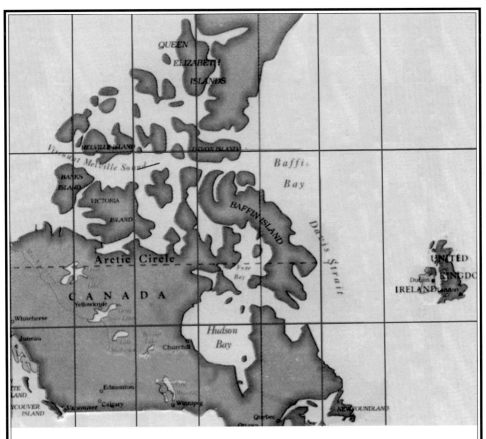

The vastness of Canada was overwhelming after living in a small country like England

About Canada

Birth of a nation 1st July 1867. The population of Canada was three million scattered over Canada's vast land mass. The French and English settlers fought to take possession of the country. The English settlers defeated the French settlers and declared Canada as an English colony.

Modern Canada has a multicultural population of 30,000,000 whose official spoken language is French and English. The Country is divided into 10 provinces and 3 territories each electing it's own Legislature and Premier. An elected Federal Parliament and Prime Minister governs Canada. Queen Elizabeth is now only a figurehead and a Government appointed Governor General attends to all Royal functions.

Chapter Four

Changing Years

A new country, a new life. The vastness of Canada was overwhelming after living in a small country like England. Toronto is a large and beautiful city. Arriving in July, the sunshine was warm creating a nice atmosphere, along with welcoming cousins who helped to quell the feeling of homesickness.

At first we rented a house temporarily while we studied house prices and investigated the different areas of the city. Martyn was working temporarily as a meter reader. He had secured this job based on advice given to him by the Registrar of the University of Toronto upon arriving in Canada the previous October. This good advice enabled him to become accustomed to Canadian life and culture. He was accepted at the University the following year. Barbara took employment in a pharmaceutical company believing this was a temporary situation. After her interview the general manager asked the personnel manager "Did you give that lady the job?" "Yes" replied the personnel manager. "I will give her one week" commented the general manager. Seventeen years later, Barbara, in her retirement speech reminded the general manager of his previous remark.

My first day teaching in Canada things did not go smoothly. Being of average height with a strong English accent and high expectations of student work ethics gave me quite a surprise. For example, one day I was writing on the chalkboard with my back to the class and I was bombarded with paper balls. Giving verbal instructions precipitated many comments from the students. Canadians pronounce 'book' as 'buck' and hang their coats on 'hucks' not 'hooks'. "How was your first day teaching in Canada?" My brother asked when he met me that evening. I explained the day's events to him and he showed his concern warning me that this was Canada and parents would sue me if I were to use corporal punishment on any student. I reassured him that my second day's teaching would likely be better. It was not. "Ask me tomorrow" was my answer to my brother's interest in my second day's teaching. Arriving to class the next day I proceeded to write on the chalkboard. I had noted the ringleader of the group and I had him under constant view. I saw the paper ball leave his hand and I met the flying object on my way to apprehend him. His feet never touched the ground until he was through the classroom door. The office door that was opposite to my classroom opened and the Technical Director demanded to know what was going on. After hearing my explanation he took the culprit into his office. Returning back to my classroom I

10, Downing Street,
London, S. W. 1.

I send my best wishes to the Winston Churchill
Collegiate Institute for the happiness and wellbeing of
those who have worked for its construction and also for those
who will profit from its guidance through many years to
come.   May good fortune attend you all.

Winston S. Churchill

found all the students busily writing notes taken from the chalkboard. Shortly after the event, the classroom door opened and the Technical Director told the culprit to sit in his seat and behave. My reaction was instant. Pushing the culprit back through the door, I informed the Technical Director that once my class was in progress, I would decide when to allow the culprit back into class. The Technical Director obviously had never encountered this kind of behaviour from a teacher before and was taken by surprise. He returned to his office taking the culprit with him, sternly informing me to report to him after class was over. I reported to his office after I had dismissed my class and was invited in. The Technical Director had his head down making notes. I waited. This short time period appeared to last a lifetime. My thoughts during this lifetime experience had me returning back home to England after the expected firing. My thoughts came to an abrupt end when the Technical Director rose from his seat with outstretched hand and asked me if I had any teacher friends in England like me; if so, he had a job for them.

I enjoyed the next seven years in the Collegiate. The Collegiate catered to a working class area of mixed races and its main emphasis was teaching trades; hair dressing, nursing cooking, gardening, dressmaking, machine shop, drafting, woodwork, electricity, bricklaying! Auto mechanics, music, printing and academics. Some ten years later government policy changed. Cutbacks and down sizing closed many of the programs. The trade school was the happiest period in my teaching career. Trade teachers were recruited from industry and were often referred to as 'not proper teachers'. They were, however, very dedicated teachers.

Canada, being a multicultural society, gave me a different social aspect. There were teachers from all walks of life; Black, Chinese, American, Ger-

Mr. Harvey:
Thanks for being a cool teacher. Your generosity and approachability has been overwhelming, and will be missed at the school. I hope you enjoy a nice retirement and always remain in good health.
Your student and buddy,
Dennis Bolic /s

man, French, Jamaican, Irish, English, Scottish, and Welsh. The student body was just as mixed; there was no religion aspect in the school. The national anthem 'O Canada', was played each day when school began. The size of the school also took some getting used to; fourteen hundred students and each student had their own locker. There were eighty teachers, all of whom had cars. This meant a large car park. The students' car park was considerably larger. I recall a funny incident when I was being introduced to each staff member. When introduced to the German teacher, he remarked "Englander, remember we came second twice". He became a close friend and was a wonderful teacher.

Looking for a home some months after our arrival in Canada did pose a problem. Money was in short supply due to government restrictions, which would not allow us to transfer our capital for a period of four years. Our Canadian bank agreed that we could borrow funds on condition that we sign a release paper confirming that any monies in our English account would be transferred to our Canadian bank when the four year waiting period was over. Having found a house in a nice area, we required furniture and household items. We had sold or given away all our belongings in England, which was a mistake. Renting a container and shipping them to Canada from England would have saved us money. All our household possessions were taken for granted and little value placed upon them. Not having a tin opener or a toilet roll holder brings life to a halt.

Settling into life's routine in our first Canadian home was now underway. Making a house a home included painting and decorating, landscaping and a host of other things. Being new to the area, friends had to be made and a new life was in the making. Several months into our new life, I was confronted with a teachers' strike. Should I join the strike? What about the mortgage and furniture loans? The strike, which occurred in January and February, taught me about Canadian winters. I had never been so cold for so long. The prolonged strike and no salary had the bank manager calling me to his office, insisting that I make payments on my mortgage. Again I was trapped. The house was sold and I was back living in my brother's basement and on Barbara's salary. The house that my brother owned had fifty acres of land. If we could divide the land, I could build a house and save money. The land was divided and I was working full-time during the week and building a house on Saturdays and Sundays.

The house took eighteen months to build. How I missed the weekenders. I employed part-time workers and sub-contracted such jobs as bricklaying and concrete pouring. Building in Canada is different from building in England. Canadian winters are long and extremely cold, and therefore a 'shell' must be built that gives some protection against the outside weather. During the winter months, inside work is carried out; inside wall structures roughing in plumbing runs, electrical work and insulation is installed.

Moving into our new home did not require professional movers, just lifting and carrying our belongings next door. I looked forward to landscaping the site, but black flies and mosquitoes made outside work intolerable. Our new home was thirty-seven miles from my school and the pharmaceutical company where Barbara worked. Large cars and excellent roads made long distance travelling

commonplace in Canada. Travelling during the summer months was fine, but during the winter months driving could become a nightmare.

Living in the country changes lifestyles. We experienced snowmobiling, cross country skiing and snow clearing. Some snowstorms leave two or more feet of snow on driveways. However, snowploughs worked all night long to clear highways of snow by morning. Summers in Canada are short with lots of sunshine and warm temperatures making outdoor swimming pools desirable. The vastness of Canada and the U.S.A. makes planning summer vacations a challenge.

It was not long before I had plans to satisfy my ever-busy mind. A new idea emerged; I sent to England for trailer suspensions, paid for them from my English bank account and had them exported to me. This was a legal loophole in the government's monetary restrictions. Buying the necessary equipment, welding machine, drilling machine and power cut-off machine, I was in production building trailers but again I missed the Weekenders'.

During my early engineering training, I had joined The Professional Institution of Production Engineers. The Institution was granted Royal Charter 13th May 1965. Being a member is important to keep up with the rapid technological changes. To become a member one had to have served an apprenticeship in Production Engineering, followed by several years in the trade and to have held a position of responsibility. Academic standard was the

Higher National Certificate. Members became Chartered Engineers and were entitled to use MIProdE C Eng after their name. After the 1939-1945 war, advancement in technological changes saw plastics replacing metals and wood, computers were used in designing and controlling machine tools and robots replacing human beings. When I emigrated to Canada I transferred my membership to the Canadian section and attended meetings. I soon became part of the executive committee, taking the position of Secretary. Seventeen years later I was appointed President of the Canadian Council. In 1991 the Institution of Production Engineers and the Institution of Electrical Engineers amalgamated (The Institution of Production Engineers became the manufacturing section of The Institution of Electrical Engineers). Michael Faraday, born 22nd September 1791, who discovered 'electromagnetic induction', is recognized as the Father of Electricity by the Institution of Electrical Engineers, which was formed in 1871. The Institution of Electrical Engineers was granted Royal Charter in 1921. In 1995 I was elected Chairman of the Institution of Electrical Engineers, Toronto Centre. I am very proud of my professional achievements. It's a long way from the early years as an apprentice at Rolls Royce.

Trailer suspensions became my speciality item. I was approached by a trailer manufacturer to supply him with eleven thousand dollars worth of suspensions, which Martyn and I delivered to his home. The agreement between the manufacturer and myself was a cheque upon delivery of the suspension units. The agreement was not kept. I was told I could collect the cheque the follow-

ing day. Arriving to collect the cheque, I was told that the manufacturer was out of town. After a number of visits, I was finally given the cheque and immediately took it to my bank, requesting that the cheque be watched closely, and that I be informed immediately if it was N.S.F. ('not-sufficient funds'). Several days passed and no word from the bank. Arriving home from school and checking my mail, a letter from the bank had finally arrived, stating that the cheque was 'N.S.F.'. Waiting for darkness, I drove to the house where we had delivered the units and checked the garage doors. The units were still on the floor where we had left them. I persuaded Martyn to drive to the house very early that morning, before the trailer manufacturer was awake, to help load the units back onto our truck. Leaving home at five am we set out for our

destination. Martyn, who was very concerned about the plan, stopped the truck and refused to proceed. He feared that we would be arrested for 'breaking and entering'. Eventually, I agreed to go to the nearest police station to discuss our plight. With the police officer's consent, Martyn and I drove to the manufacturer's house and noisily aroused him. Speaking loudly, I told him that his cheque was N.S.F. and giving him the police officer's card, I assured him that steps were being taken to lay charges for fraud. The commotion brought his wife and two small children to the scene. His wife, learning of the affair, demanded that the units be given back. Several minutes later, the manufacturer helped Martyn and I to load the units onto our vehicle.

Four years had passed since we emigrated and our English funds were released to our Canadian bank. The amount was a shock. Four years earlier, the exchange rate was two dollars and thirty cents for the sterling pound. Now we received one dollar eighty-eight cents for our pound, losing almost two-sevenths or our life's savings.

Buying a house in the vicinity of the Collegiate

Living outside the big city has advantages and disadvantages. Advantages include less traffic problems, cleaner air, as well as peace and quiet. Having lived in the home I built for seven years, we decided that there were too many disadvantages. The long distance travelling to and from work extended our workday by two hours and having one car made separate schedules impossible. Barbara and I decided to sell.

Buying a house in the vicinity of the collegiate in which I taught and which was close to Barbara's workplace relieved stress and gave us more time to do things not possible when we lived in the country. We became members of a ten-pin bowling league and bought season theatre tickets. Black flies and mosquitoes were gone and that was a bonus. Gardening was a pleasure once again. Shortly after moving, I was upgraded to Assistant Technical Director at another collegiate, which was named after my wartime hero, Winston Churchill. I enjoyed teaching at this school until my retirement at the age of sixty-five years. Where had the years gone? I had been in the workforce for fifty-one years with only a few days off for sickness, and this accomplishment I attribute to having good health. Smoking, taking drugs, alcoholism and bad diet shortens lives and lowers the quality of life.

Most Canadian houses have a basement. The bungalow above has a basement equal to the upper floor area. Roofs are low pitched and covered with ashpalt shingles.

I sold the trailer business after retiring from teaching, and a local engineering company hired me as a part-time estimator. This part-time position along with Barbara's retirement enabled us to become 'snowbirds'. Snowbirds are people who leave the snow areas in the north and move south to sunny, warm regions for the winter months.

A sad loss to me during this period was losing my twin sister whom I loved and admired. Looking back on her life, it appears to me that some human beings have lots of 'bad luck' and others ' good luck'. This phenomenon puzzles me. Is our destiny preprogrammed or self-programmed? My sister became pregnant at seventeen and homeless, she moved in with her boyfriend's family who loved her and were very kind to her. They married and their first daughter was born. Her husband died of cancer shortly after their second daughter was born. I am reminded that I have only one brother living from the family where it all began for me.

Employment in Canada was becoming difficult to find and the economic outlook was not good. Employers used new terms to inform their employees that their services were no longer required. In my younger days employers were more abrupt. 'People were 'fired', 'sacked', or sent to the office 'to collect one's final pay packet'. There were no comebacks on the employer. Today, however, the employer must have a good reason or be prepared to face a court

Part of the tradditional Pottery making process, pouring slip into a mould.

of inquiry regarding the dismissal. The new terms are 'downsizing', 'cutting-back' and 're-structuring', which are not so abrupt; however, the results are the same. Unfortunately, today the age of fifty can make you too old to be employed. The best chance for employment after you reach the age of fifty is upgrading or learning new skills. My part-time employment eventually was 'down-sized' and for the first time, I actually had nothing to do apart from gardening, house maintenance, and being involved with my two grandsons. Martyn, now a single parent, lives next door to us. Where have all the years gone? I wondered as we planned the celebration of fifty years of marriage.

Through my association with the Engineering society, I was asked to design an aromatherapy warmer to dispense fragrance oils into the air. Designing the warmer involved making ceramic bowls. I was back in business and amazingly, Barbara became a fulltime employed retiree. By manufacturing the warmers, I became a 'potter' making ceramic bowls. Ceramics are made in many ways. One method is called 'throwing'. It is slow and expensive, utilizing a revolving potters' wheel where wet clay is shaped to the required design by hand. When quantities are required, moulds are used. Liquid clay is poured into the mould. This method is called 'pouring'. The aromatherapy warmers were a success, orders increased and the part time venture grew into a full time business. The warmers are sold exclusively to one company who distributes them throughout Canada and Japan. A catalogue company contacted me requesting a price to decorate three thousand plates. The price I quoted was accepted and more production time had to be found if the delivery date was to be honoured. I hired temporary part-time help and the order was delivered on time. The temporary part-time help still remains with us after several years and thousands of decorated plates. Being a 'potter' gave me lots of new terms: slip (liquid clay), green ware, (dried liquid clay), bisque, (fired greenware), glaze, (applied to bisque ware to seal the porous bisque surface), decal, (transfer when applied to a glaze surface and heated to 1400 degrees F. The decal design melts into the liquid glaze and becomes a permanent design on the ceramic piece). Decals are produced from original artwork and produced in large numbers, making cheap copies of the original.

Throwing a vessel on a potter's wheel

Working on repetitive productions can be boring and often boredom is broken by 'thinking' or letting the mind 'wander' into 'thoughts' from the past. Where have all the years gone? The answers are in memories. Memories are incredible because in a few moments a life is relived.

I recall so many images and events that have taken place in my lifetime such as cycling to work, the horse-drawn hearse, horse-drawn milk and coal deliveries, collecting of rags and bones. Massey's bone works situated on Silverdale Road. Newcastle made glue. Depending upon the direction of the wind either Newcastle or Silverdale had to put up with the smell. I remember the steam-driven lorries, tram car running on steel tracks, joining the crowds to see our first horseless carriage, zeppelins in the sky, metal boxes (radios) that had valves, dry and wet batteries and a long wire running up a high pole which when turned on thrilled us all to hear voices or music coming from its speakers.

After 1939 technology increased rapidly because of the demands of the World War. The slow relaxed and supposedly moral Victorian society changed into a world measured by material wealth and rapid technology advancement while moral standards steadily declined. These days, cycling is done mainly for health and enjoyment. Walking is still a necessity but

12-123. Clothes Pins, good grade hardwood at a low price.
3 dozen clothes pins. **10d**

12-129. Clothes Line, of sisal rope, 80 feet long; for use where space is limited.
Price............ **10d**

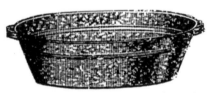

13-977. Galvanized iron Foot Bath or Rinsing Tub, is strongly made and non-rustable, oval shape. It will be found a handy article Depth 7¾ ins., length 20¾ ins.; width 15½ ins.........**7/6d**

ZINC

GRANITE

mainly for health reasons. Mail, newspaper deliveries and advertising flyers (referred to as junk mail) are the only regular home deliveries that take place today. Automobiles have taken over delivery services and horses have fallen victim to 'downsizing'. Crowds no longer gather to see the horseless carriages, which stifle and pollute the atmosphere, killing and maiming thousands every year. The modern horseless carriages are slick and unlike their predecessors, having speedometers, window wipers, oil gauges, water temperature gauges, directional signals, air-conditioning, powered windows, power locks and cruise control. Cars have turned roads and open spaces into parking lots. Hot air balloons fascinate onlookers just as zeppelins fascinated onlookers in the yesteryears. Airliners carrying hundreds of passengers are heard more easily than seen, as they travel at speeds in excess of five hundred miles per hour and heights of thirty thousand feet across the globe.

Space travel is now a reality. Overcoming the required scientific knowledge of breaking free from earth's gravity is history. Landing on the moon is also history. Building space stations, walking in space and sending rockets to distant stars is a far cry from the Wright brothers' first flight. Telecommunications today have progressed from the early radio messages sent by Marconi to fax messages reaching across the world instantly. The younger generation today grow up with television, computers, calculators, videos and take no heed that the high volume they must listen to will in the future require them to wear a high-tech device, namely the hearing aid.

People living in modern homes no longer use 'dolly tubs and dolly pegs' to do their laundry, nor do they buy blocks of ice to keep food storage cold. Central vacuum cleaners have replaced dustpans and brushes. Electric light switches replaced matches. In the kitchen, electric stoves, microwave ovens, refrigerators and plastic coated working surfaces have replaced the stoneware sink and wooden tables. Coal fires have been replaced with central heating and water heaters. Carpeted and vinyl floors, double glazing, vertical blinds and chandeliers have given antique value to home furnishing, which I see in my memories.

Appendicitis, sugar diabetes, smallpox and tuberculosis meant certain death. Millions of human beings spent much of their lives in darkness because of cataracts. I myself had cataracts removed and plastic lenses inserted. Many think that cataracts grow on the outside of the eye. Cataracts are the deterioration of the lens inside of the eye, which becomes opaque. The opaque lens is removed and a clear plastic lens is replaced. It was the most wonderful event in my life for me, having been partially blind my entire life. Being a vain person, looks were most important to me and I refused to wear glasses. This caused me lots of problems. I was overjoyed to have contact lenses fitted in 1946 by George McKellen, whose optician shop was located on the corner of Merrial Street and High Street in Newcastle. The first contact lens could only be worn for a period of two hours because the lens covered the eye completely and deprived the eye of oxygen. I still have the original lenses, which measure 25mm in diameter. A suction cup was required to remove these giant plastic lenses. The Guinness Book of Records informed me that another person had worn his contact lenses two years longer than I had. I had no ill effect after wearing the lenses for forty-four years. Back in the thirties, a life span was sixty years for healthy people. Today, so many people enjoy good health into their eighties, even after being given a second chance through heart surgery. Doubters in Dr. Barnard's first heart transplant now hail his success.

Although human behaviour is influenced mainly by the family environment, other influences may change or add either positive or negative behaviours. Children's behaviour never fails to amaze me. Where do they learn this behaviour? Is it from their parents, peers, teachers, television programs, and films in the home, schools, and workplace? Being fat, disfigured, handicapped, homosexual, lesbian, black, different religion and a host of other reasons motivates violence. As I have travelled though life, violence has always been present, if not for one reason then for another. However, always influenced by human behaviour, I am convinced that violence is within all of us, but, those who came into life surrounded by violence or abuse are at high risk of continuing the pattern.

Abuse comes in many forms; sexual, mental and emotional. Often family abuse is difficult to detect or when detected, is difficult to prove.

Memories make me realize how deeply ingrained my character became. It was formed by early life experiences. In the past students feared or respected teachers. Educators ruled with an 'iron fist' using corporal or other forms of punishment. The 'Young Offenders Act' does not allow prosecution of children under the age of twelve years, even for serious crimes. Churches constantly reminded their flock that damnation befalls defaulters. In the past this held many marriages together. Having made the commitment "for as long as we live', divorce was out of the question for couples. Leaving your partner brought scorn upon those who chose this course. The 21st Century brings immense changes for society. Many religious congregations have significantly decreased in numbers. Some faiths have relaxed and changed their laws, allowing divorcees to remarry, practising birth control and admitting homosexuals and lesbians into their faiths. Smoking and alcoholism were the accepted scourges in the thirties. I recall walking with a friend through the village, just to look at an elderly lady smoking (much to her neighbours' disgust) a clay tobacco pipe and drinking beer. Those of us who did not drink or smoke (there were a few of us) were viewed as abnormal. Married couples stayed together for life and ladies promised to 'obey'. As we approach the new millennium couples live common-law and some marry later for the children's sake, or they may change partners a number of times during their lifetime. Couple now refers to two males, two females or one male and one female. Changing partners and out of control sexual behaviour has brought wrath on the human race in a disease called 'aids'. Unfortunately, through blood transfusion many innocent people have become innocent victims.

Chapter Five

Reflections

Through my memories I can compare the distant past to the immediate past and assess the changes that have taken place. For instance, from my distant past I recall 'fighting rival gangs for no other reason than we belonged to the Church of England faith and they were Roman Catholics'. In my immediate past, I recall working in harmony with people of different races and faiths. Perhaps the saying "you cannot put old heads on young shoulders" accurately illustrates that life's experiences reflect and mould character.

Important qualities, values and attitudes we learn from our character-forming years include belonging, love, respect and patience. The human race benefits from belonging to family, friends, communities and societies. Without love this life can fall apart, resulting in unhappiness. Love forms happy family life and guides us to becoming healthy people. Respect creates harmony within the family, friendships, communities and societies. Consideration earns respect from those close to us, making for a life of contentment.

Who did I become? The answer to this question is ever-changing. At different times in our lives the answer will be different. Life's experiences or in-experiences form our different values. 'We belong to the Church of England faith and our rivals are Roman Catholics'. Where did we learn that? Hate and prejudices cut deep grooves inside the human race, often resulting in terrible conflict or wars. As we grow older, we 'mellow' and hopefully come to understand the importance of values like, belonging, love, respect and patience. All becomes part of our character.

As we travel through life, we learn to adjust to every-day stresses. For me, I have practised and benefited from 'doing it now' rather than 'later' or 'soon'. Perhaps the saying "tomorrow never comes" derives from such situations. In our household, preparing meals, cleaning, shopping, gardening and a host of other things are required for an efficient and happy existence. All the family takes part in carrying through the chores, unlike some cultures that have the women treated no better than slaves. I am sure that I was taught good healthy habits in my early life. Never take things for granted, otherwise many disappointments will have to be borne. Taking heed to health warnings will help to give a good quality of life. Watching our intake of fat, not smoking, exercising and a drug-free life will lengthen our life span. Hasty decisions should be avoided. It encourages each of us to 'think again' or 'give it a second thought' before making our final decision. Making a bad decision can be painful and long. There is no going back. I have learned to solve my problems by considering them just before I fall asleep. Amazingly, when I awaken, I have formulated a solution in my head. It is apparent that many famous people have benefited greatly by their understanding of these basic life values. Ultimately they have helped the entire human race. What would we do without electricity? British scientist, Michael Faraday, discovered 'Electromagnetic Induction' which led to the continuous generation of electrical power. Electricity, which is readily available at the turn of a switch, is the result of Faraday's discovery. American scientist, Thomas Edison invented the electric light bulb along with many other inventions. Both became involved in developing this wonderful phenomenon and between them gave us the electricity as we know it today. I decided to survey an average day's involvement with electricity. I awakened to my electric alarm clock. It is very cold outside but the house is nice and warm, thanks to the electric heating. Taking a warm shower, I appreciate the electric water heating system. Dressing in clean garments, I was thankful for the electric washer, dryer and iron. Preparing breakfast, I boil water in an electric kettle and cook my cereal in the microwave oven. The telephone signals that someone wants to talk to me. The list is endless. Our lives have become dependent on electricity. Thanks to Faraday and Edison, our quality of life improved drastically from the days before electricity.

"Where have all the years gone?", is a question queried by so many of us. Is it because the years pass us by and we are too busy to notice their passing? Do the years go faster as we grow older? Or is it because we are always fighting the clock or there just are not enough hours in the day? Time rolls on regardless and we have to live with it. Monday again!! Winter is here already!! My memory reminds me how much time has passed me by. Princess Elizabeth became Queen Elizabeth II on February 2nd, 1952. Russia's 'Sputnik I' was launched, making them first in space on October 4th, 1957. I recall watching it pass over as a faint light in the sky. I recall the shock with the news in November 1963 that President John F. Kennedy had been shot dead in Dallas, Texas. Famous names John Paul, Ringo and George, better known as 'The Beatles', were climbing the charts, the year, 1963. Sir Winston Churchill, Britain's wartime leader and hero died in January 1965. Landing on the moon in July 1969,

Thomas Edison was born in 1847 and died in 1931. Edison spent most of his 84 years inventing or discovering several thousand different products. The electric light bulb was perhaps his greatest invention, which benefitted mankind the most. He invented electric sockets, switches, meters, wax paper, tin foil, the phonograph and the list is endless.

Visiting Fort Myers, Florida it is evident that the area was built around this world renowned scientist.

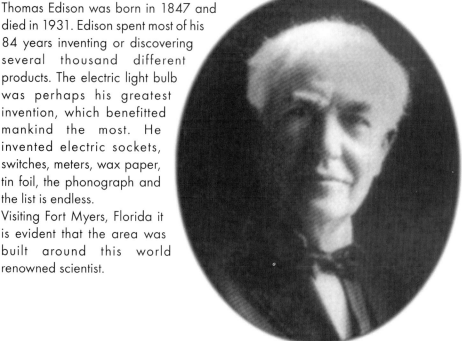

Thomas Edison

Michael Faraday was born 22nd September 1791 in Southwark. Faraday served an apprenticeship as a bookbinder, it was here that he read books on chemistry. Electricity at that time was a branch of chemistry. Michael attended lectures on electricity given by Sir Humphry Davy the famous chemist. Later he sent his own notes to Davy and requested a job at the Royal Institution. Davy made him his assistant. Faraday embarked on a scientific career and became one of the world's greatest scientists.

MICHAEL FARADAY

Michael Faraday

American astronauts, Neil Armstrong and Edwin Aldrin were the first human beings to set foot on the moon. The first heart transplant was performed by Christian Barnard in South Africa on the 25th of July, 1971. 'The Peoples Princess', Diana marries Prince Charles on the 29th of July, 1981. All these events are now history. Recalling them makes me wonder, 'Where have all the years gone?'

The world changed dramatically during the 20th century, due to unparalleled advances in technology and countless scientific discoveries. Inventions such as the telephone, computer, automobile, aeroplane and discoveries of electricity and penicillin have vastly improved our quality of life. The 21st century heralds new opportunities and challenges to all who advance into the new millennium.

The American Civil War started basically over the cause of slavery. Northerners saw the slave auctions where men, women and children were bid for like cattle, to be evil. Often families were broken up as their members were sold to separate buyers.

Abraham Lincoln, elected minority President in 1860, gave the fire branding members in the south their excuse for secession. Jefferson Davis, who was declared the first President of the Confederacy, was now faced with the task of shaping a new nation and waging a defensive war.

From the horror of the conflict, where brother fought against brother, cities ravaged, villages and farms destroyed, emerged a new Union with a new constitution for all it's citizens. This Union became the United States of America.

January 15th, 1901, as the century was rung in, the extent of Britain's imperial power had never been greater. The Empire, stretching around the globe, has one heart, one head, one language and one policy, stated one national newspaper. Looking back to the beginning of the previous century, the picture was far gloomier. Napoleon's meteoric rise was just the beginning. The American Civil War cost an average of four hundred and thirty soldiers killed daily during four years of bloody battles. The Boer War had just started and so had the fight against the Dutch who refused to recognize the 'Just Sovereignty of Queen Victoria'. The French Revolution was underway, changing the French society. Diseases that were prevalent would reach epidemic proportions. Gravediggers worked day and night. The Twentieth Century saw two World Wars, followed by a period of rapid technological change. Computers and robots were developed. TV and radio entered every household. Global warming appears to be a reality. H.G. Wells wrote science fiction on space travel. Today space travel is almost routine, changing Wells's fiction to prophecy. George Orwell's 1984 novel depicting 'Big Brother' had no experience of Social Security numbers computer data banks or DNA testing. Even so, he predicted 'Big Brother'.

Beacons of light became permanent fixtures on our mind. Unexpectedly, lights go out, as did the Russian Empire. Not only did its lights go out, but also its beacon collapsed. The British Empire's light is still waning. All the great countries, which were under the British rule at the turn of the century (Canada, India, Australia and New Zealand), are now independent. Hong Kong was handed back to China as promised after ninety-nine years. Ireland is all but gone. Scotland and Wales seek home rule. Will the Royal family survive or will television and the media be their demise? The Peoples' Princess Diana, would have assured the monarchy's future into the 21st century. Terrorism has reached the stage where no one is out of reach from the thugs who hide in the darkness of martyrdom, willing to sacrifice the innocent and themselves. Two thousand years have passed and still the battles are being fought in the area where the 'Prince of Peace' was born. In a world where incredible strides forward have been made, why this stagnation? Is it human greed and we have no control over it?

If we have no control over our greed, and greed appears to be the cause of most of our human problems, then what hope is there for the future of mankind? When the human race was created, was this the beginning of the path of self-destruction because greed is part of our makeup? We are told that if a future world war were fought using hydrogen bombs (which probably would be controlled from space stations), it would cause mass destruction to cities, continents and more importantly, our atmosphere. Do the forces of good override the forces of evil? If so, then there is hope and a future for mankind.

Recalling from my early memories, in the nineteen thirties, the common cold, influenza, measles, chicken pox, small pox, pneumonia, scarlet fever, diphtheria, tuberculosis, silicosis, tonsillitis, mumps and appendicitis were prevalent. Common disabling illnesses included asthma, cataract, glaucoma, rheumatism, polio, St. Vitas dance, epileptic seizures, thyroid and many skin and blood disorders.

During the nineteenth century medical technology advanced rapidly. Drugs and antibiotics in the form of tablets, capsules, and intravenous, have eliminated many of these illnesses and given relief to many sufferers. I recall in the 1930s 'Aspro' (packed in strips) was the common pain reliever and cold cure. My mother would give to us hot lemonade and two aspro tablets for any ailment. Continuous uses of aspirin developed stomach problems. Sixty years later we still do not have a cure for the common cold. Perhaps the cure alludes us because there are over two hundred different viruses that produce similar cold-like symptoms. Common colds usually last seven days, varying from person to person. I rarely get a cold, probably one in five years and I tell my family "I am too busy to get a cold".

Inoculation and vaccinations give protection against many diseases. Influenza and pneumonia shots are given to the elderly. Blood thinning tablets are prescribed for those with high blood cholesterol. The medical profession in the 1990s is concerned about the appearance of 'super' viruses. The most serious is the 'flesh' eating virus. Thinking back over the years, my health problem was kidney stones. Several brothers and my son suffer too from kidney stones. The pain is very severe. Drinking eight glasses of water daily appears to be the remedy. I was born very shortsighted and later in life I developed cataracts. These were removed and implants inserted. This was the most wonderful thing that ever happened to me in my lifetime. Great strides have been made regarding cataracts. Back in the 1950s removal of cataracts was an operation that meant hospitalisation for several days. The patient had to lie perfectly still with pillows placed each side of the head for

support. When the eye healed, glasses were fitted. The lens of the glasses was very thick (referred to as bottle tops) and very heavy. The cataract operation was only performed when the lens was 'ripe' (the lens had become opaque), after a period of six to twelve months and the eye had developed a cataract. It would then be operated on. Today's technology has changed cataract surgery. Today, patients have the cataracts removed, implants inserted and leave the hospital immediately. An operation can be performed on the other eye within days, if necessary.

Many wonderful discoveries have taken place during the twentieth century; insulin discovered by Frederick Banting in the year 1922, Penicillin discovered by Sir Alexander Fleming in the year 1928, but not used on humans until 1941, X-ray discovered by Wilhelm K. Roentgen in the year 1895. Since Dr. Barnard's first heart transplant in 1971, transplants involving kidneys, liver and lungs have become commonplace. It is no surprise to meet people who have had a heart by-pass, aneurysm-ectomy, hip replacement, kneecap replacement, bowel resection or a prostrate gland removed.

In the workforce, technology has changed the workplace. Modern production plants are clean, well lit, and ventilated, with no overhead shafts, belts, and pulleys. Gone are the pot-heating stoves and gaslights.

Steel girders that give wide spans and supports have allowed architects to plan open concepts to modern workplaces. Windows, from my memories, were small with lots of support to secure the glass, yet today we see high-rise office towers built completely of glass and stainless steel. Silent elevators

have replaced flights of stairs. Telephones, computers, intercoms, and high-tech materials have replaced heavy wooden desks, cupboards, walls, doors, lighting and ceilings.

Travel may affect each of us differently. Driving our car to the airport, parking it, and boarding a jetliner to our destination may be our travel mode. Using our car to travel daily to our workplace, catching a bus, subway, or train, is the transport means for thousands of people. City dwellers may walk or cycle to work. In my memory is Duggins Bus Service that ran between Silverdale and Newcastle. During the day when few people travelled, the company ran an eighteen seat 'little' Safety Coach. During 'rush' hours it was replaced with a thirty-two seat 'big' Safety Coach. In the 1930s in Silverdale, Dixie Dean and Mr. Ellis, long-time drivers of these coaches and 'conductor' Ernie Peak, will be remembered. How would people from the eighteenth century react to the changes?

Recalling my early memories of the retail shops in the village of Silverdale, many names come to mind. The co-ops stores in Victoria Street, Crown Bank, and High Street (on the corner of Kinsey Street). The Co-op stores gave cash dividends related to the amount spent during each quarter. I can remember lining up each quarter to collect the dividend, 'divy', which my mother was in

Frederick Banting (right) discovered Insulin in 1922. The discovery earned him a Nobel prize in medicine. Banting served as a medical officer in the 1914 -18 war and was awarded the Military Cross for his heroic services on the battlefields in France. He worked at the University of Toronto where he discovered insulin. Banting was killed in a plane crash in 1941 when he was flying to England to co-ordinate research between Canada and Britain.

Alexander Fleming (left) born in Scotland, discovered Penicillin in 1928, the wonder drug. Fleming was awarded the Nobel Prize for medicine and Knighted for his services. Fleming served in the British army in the 1914 - 18 war as a medical officer.

Wilhelm Roentgen (right) discovered X-ray in 1895. Scientists never know when a great discovery will occur. This was the case when Roentgen noticed a glow when he was carrying out some experiments. He had discovered X-ray and became a world famous scientist as a result of his work.

need of. The dividend would usually amount to six shillings and three pence. Other retail shops were Jack Lowe's grocer stores, Hampton and Allman butcher shops, Barratt and Holden cycle shops, Hall's battery charging shop, and Lowndes confectionery shop. All these businesses were on Church Street. I can remember staring in Pepper's candy store window and deciding what to buy with my tuppence pocket money. Of course the English staple food, fish and chips, was well catered for in Silverdale by Rhodes, Daniels and Wilkinsons. The locals would debate who made the best 'chips'. The best ice cream in

'Corner Shops' were on every street corner in Silverdale in the 1930's, but during the 1940's the larger businesses began to take over. These larger businesses brought in bulk, or sold products produced in third world countries, whose low labour costs could not be matched.

Silverdale and the surrounding district was made by 'Mussy' Valco on Crown Bank. Who else could make ice cream better than an Italian? Purchasing Plant's 'oatcakes' meant lining up either Saturday evening or early Sunday mornings. Bacon, sausage and egg rolled up in an oatcake gave the best Sunday breakfast ever tasted. Two local newsagents, Morrall and Steadman found work for the young, delivering newspapers each morning. The evening 'Sentinel' was sold in the streets by boys and girls calling out loudly.

Smelling the bread baking at Bird's and Madock's bakeries made us feel hungry. Builders Philips and G.K. Downing supplied building materials and built many of Silverdale's homes. Houses built by G.K. Downings can still be recognized by their shiny red brick and yellow single insert bricks around the windows and doorways. Houses in May Street and Kinsey Street were built by them. To have a tooth 'pulled' meant seeing Mr. Barratt. Barbers, Norcup and

A Modern Day Supermarket - Buying in bulk, the small corner shops could not compete.

Harrison cut men's hair for as long as I can remember. The ladies had to book days ahead for their hair 'do' with Mrs. Kendrick. The local undertaker was Douglas Ryder. Silverdale in my memories was a thriving community, but the days for the small shopkeepers were numbered. The saying "Big fish swallow up the small fish" eventually took place. Large business concerns with their quantity buying and bright well laid out stores, out-priced the corner shopkeepers and most were forced to close.

Silverdale's Post office catered for savings, money exchange services, and postal services. The nearest bank was located in Newcastle, but in the 1930s not many Silverdale people required bank services. My first week's wage was seven shillings and sixpence, with stoppages amounting to fourpence, leaving seven shillings and twopence in the small brown envelope. Wages were paid out in cash on Friday afternoon. All members of our family gave to our mother the brown envelope. In my case, from the first week's wage, mother handed me one shilling and twopence for pocket money. Most weeks, I would go to the post office and bank sixpence into my post office savings. Postal orders were the method of sending money via the post and the stamp would cost one halfpenny.

Wm. Tagg Foundry and Fitting Shop, Sutton Street, Newcastle under lyme. The Author worked in Tagg's fitting shop for six months in 1939. The Hidden dangers in the shops were numerous. No safety glasses, hard hats, work boots or canteen facilities. In comparison a mordern production plant like the one below is spacious, well organised, clean, well lit, heated, airconditioned and ventilated. Safety rules must be obeyed, wearing eye protection, work boots and hard hats. Canteens, first aid rooms and toilet facilities must be provided.

During the war, salaries increased, and banking began to be a more appropriate method for dealing with money transactions. After the war, banking became international and methods of immediate transactions were required. Banks merged internationally. New types of banking emerged, namely Visa and MasterCard. Plastic cards were introduced to purchase items or cash (using banking machines) anywhere in the world. Workers salaries were paid directly into their bank accounts.

Considering my past seventy years and wondering where the years have gone, I realize that my son and grandsons feel it's forever in time, just as I did about my parents and grandparents. How then, can we understand the universe and its formation? Our earth was born millions of years ago and I wonder where my brief seventy years have gone.

"Where do we go from here?" This question must have been asked in the year 1899. One hundred years later, our fore-bearers would remark "incredible". Over the changes that will take place by the year 2099 our grandchildren will remark "cool". In the early centuries with no news media or transport, the world was large, with little knowledge and life was slow. Little change took place in the hundred-year cycle. I doubt if the question, "Where have all the years gone?" would have been asked.

Many dramatic changes took place during the 20th century. The world population was 1.6 billion. Queen Victoria died in 1901 after reigning for 64 years. In 1914 Archduke Ferdinand of Austria was assassinated and World War One erupted. Russia was in turmoil and Lenin lead the working class into a bloody revolution. Czar Nicholas, his wife and family were executed and buried in unmarked graves. The great depression of 1929 plunged the world into great hardship. Governments, banks and companies went broke and unemployment spread like a plague. Germany's leader, Adolf Hitler began plans for world domination attacking Poland in 1939. Britain and France then declared war on Germany. The horrors of World War Two included the 'Holocaust in which eight million Jews were sent to the gas chambers. Cities throughout Europe were flattened and thousands died nightly. Japan bombed Pearl Harbour in 1941 bringing the United States of America into the war. Many land and sea battles were fought throughout Asia in which thousands died. The United States dropped the first atom bombs on Hiroshima and Nagasaki in 1945 and World War Two was over. In 1946 the United Nations General Assembly replaced the League of Nations which had failed in it's goal to preserve peace. Mao Tsetung proclaimed the People's Republic of China in 1949. The Vietnam War fought unsuccessfully by the U.S.A against North Vietnam ended in 1975. Communism began to crumble with the tearing down of 'The Berlin Wall' and the Soviet Union break up continued into the twenty first century.

Technology advanced throughout the 19th century and in 1901 Marconi sent the first transatlantic radio signal. In 1905 Einstein published his 'Theory of Relativity' and in 1913 Henry Ford opened his Model-T car assembly line. Commercial T.V. was born in 1941 and the moon landing in 1969 heralded man's breaking free from earth and opened up the Universe. The world population reached 6 billion.

As I end my life story, my sincere thanks go to all the people who were a part of my life experiences. Many are unnamed, many are not even acknowledged, but all have influenced me greatly. "Where have all the years gone?", I ask myself, knowing that the clock keeps ticking and with each tick, I find the answers in the form of memories, which all began when I joined the race of time.

The End

Other Books published by THREE COUNTIES PUBLISHING (Books) LTD - TCP Books, and which are all available by mail order from the publishers are: -

Policing The Potteries	By Alf Tunstall & Jeff Cowdell ISBN 0-9535239-9-3	*Price £ 17.95*
Hanley Wakes	by Derrick Woodward ISBN 0 9535239 - 8 - 5	*Price £ 7.95*
Where Have all The Year Gone	by Reg. Harvey	*Price £ 9.95*
A History of Longton	by Prof. J. H. Y. Briggs ISBN 0 9535239 - 1 - 8	*Price £14.95*
The Spirit of the Place	by M. J. W. Rogers ISBN 0 9535239 - 3 - 4	*Price £16.95*
In Name Only	by C. W. Sheldon ISBN 0 9535239 - 5 - 0	*Price £ 13.95*
Gently Thru' Life	by David Whitmore ISBN 0 9535239 - 4 - 2	*Price £ 12.95*
'A Victorian Pottery	by Peter Beckett ISBN 0 9535239 - 6 - 9	*Price £ 8.95*
'In Search of Fenton Castle'	by Barbara Maddox ISBN 0 9535239 - 7 - 7	*Price £ 8.95*

If you do not wish to order any books but would like to be sent our twice yearly newsletter on new publications please complete the address panel below and send it to us marked NEWSLETTER PLEASE

POSTAGE - PLEASE NOTE:

ORDER ONE BOOK   POSTAGE & PACKAGE ADD £ 1.50
ORDER TWO BOOKS   POSTAGE & PACKAGE ADD £ 2.75
ORDER ANY THREE BOOKS OR MORE   POSTAGE & PACKAGE ADD £ 3.95
Uk Postal rates only, for international orders pleas contact us for postage rates.

TOTAL REMITTANCE Incl. POSTAGE   **£**   **.**   **p**

Your Name ....

Address ....

....

Post Code .... Tel. No. ....(for use only if difficulty with delivery)

Cheques should be made payable to **Three Counties Publishing (Books) Ltd**
and sent to **P.O. Box 435, Leek, Staffs, ST13 5TB**
Please allow up to 10 - 21 days for delivery of books in stock.
This Order Form may be photocopied if you require more or would like to pass one to a friend